RIDE FAST

RIDE FAST

GET UP TO SPEED ON YOUR BIKE IN 10 WEEKS OR LESS · ERIC HARR

RODALE

Photographs by Will Taylor Photography

Book design by Gavin Robinson

Library of Congress Cataloging-in-Publication Data

Harr, Eric, date.
    Ride fast : get up to speed on your bike in 10 weeks or less / Eric Harr.
        p.   cm.
    Includes index.
    ISBN-13 978–1–59486–058–4 paperback
    ISBN-10 1–59486–058–0 paperback
    1. Cycling—Training.   I. Title.
    GV1048.H37   2006
    796.6—dc22   2005031185

Distributed to the trade by Holtzbrinck Publishers

2   4   6   8   10   9   7   5   3   1   paperback

To Dad—without question, the smartest person I know—whose wise words I live by. "Boy, life is: to learn to love to love to learn. Love is: to love to learn to learn to love."

To Mom—without question, the strongest person I know—who always taught me to treat everyone with equal respect.

To Alexandra—without question, the most loving person I know—who has never left my side. Never even budged.

To Owen—without question, the most loyal soul I know—who has loved me without reservation, without judgment, and without conditions.

To Vivienne—without question, the most remarkable person I know—who rescued me from cynicism and showed me how to love life again with my whole heart.

CONTENTS

ACKNOWLEDGMENTS

My good friend and a former executive editor at Rodale, Jeremy Katz, provided the instruction—and the inspiration—for this book. The instruction: Put out a title like this to help riders go fast. The inspiration: He went from 0 to 25 miles an hour on his bike in a matter of weeks. And Jeremy did it in precisely the way one should: He had fun (he's a big kid on his bike). He was smart (by following an intelligent training plan), and he did it fast. (Just getting back into shape wasn't enough for Jeremy; he wanted to see what he could do on the bike and he wanted to do it quickly.) Two weeks into his quest, I told him that he needed to be judicious with intervals; that the high-intensity stuff might wear him out too soon. Here was his response in a late-night e-mail to me: "Eric, I'm sorry. I just can't help myself on the intervals. I took some vitamin C [he was feeling ill], felt better, and attacked some short intervals tonight. Eight sets of 40 seconds on, 2½ minutes off. I think I must have gotten close to my max heart rate because on the last two, I thought I was going to barf. The sick thing? I loved it. I was so pumped at the end of it, I wrote a presentation/strategic plan for my group. Here it is 11:20 p.m., and I'm still too jazzed to sleep!" Jeremy's unbridled love of the bike, his passion for riding fast, and the childlike innocence he recaptured are emotions and experiences I want you to tap into as you read this book.

INTRODUCTION

When was the last time you rode your bicycle? No, I mean *really* rode your bicycle. When did you saddle up with wild eyes, a fire in your belly (and coffee in your veins!), and, on a sparkling day, motor over your favorite route with seemingly endless fuel and power in your legs?

Has it been too long?

If you're like most cyclists, you've probably been doing a decent job of staying in shape and squeezing in your "weekend rides" (weather, family, and social schedule permitting, of course). If you're like most cyclists, you also wish you could ride more and with more skill, speed, and stamina.

You know you have more in you to give. You can feel it. It's like a glowing ember deep in your belly; it's a spark that is now ready to be fanned and stoked into a full, fiery blaze.

There was probably a time in your life—maybe it was a few months ago, perhaps it was a few years—when you felt this way about your cycling. You were on fire. You may have been on the bike 4, 5, or even 6 days a week. Your pedal stroke felt silky smooth, effortless—there were no dead spots in there! When you threw your leg over the top tube and rolled out of your driveway, a smile swept over your face—and a feeling of freedom and childlike innocence swept over you—as your cares and concerns were left behind.

Out on the road, you felt strong and resilient on those windy flat stretches, mighty on the climbs, and sure-pedaled on the descents. You could access your "zone" more easily, and you could stay in it for longer periods of time.

You might have even felt a Zenlike, otherworldly "oneness" with your bicycle. (Okay, maybe that's going a bit too far, but you get my drift.)

On a bicycle, when your body seamlessly and without effort follows the will and desire of your mind, it's a thrilling feeling.

Don't you think it's time to get that feeling back?

That's what this book is about.

In these pages, I'm going to show you how to take your cycling up a notch (or 2, or 5, or 10 . . . the number of notches is entirely up to you!). I'm going to lay out a series of easy-to-implement strategies and a terrific, detailed program—all of which is designed to help you pour more power into your pedals and put more passion into your cycling.

The thrill of riding a bicycle is one of life's wholesome joys. The natural buzz you get riding your bike swiftly, carving in and out over beautiful terrain, and doing it with strength, grace, efficiency—and a fire in your belly—is a feeling that resonates in the childlike part of your heart regardless of age, background, or gender.

Cycling is also a great way to get healthier and live a better life.

Cycling is one of the most enjoyable, beneficial, and popular physical activities in the world. Whatever your fitness goal, a bicycle is the ideal tool to achieve it.

"The sport of cycling is a bonanza for your health, well-being, and performance," says Mark McCarthy, PhD, an exercise specialist with the British Medical Association in London. "It improves cardiovascular health and joint functioning, reduces body fat and stress, and decreases the risk of an array of health-related ailments such as osteoporosis, osteoarthritis, and diabetes. Cycling also has a nice community element to it and allows you to enjoy more scenery with greater ease," says Dr. McCarthy.

When we were kids, we *loved* our bikes. When we rode, nothing could pierce our reverie—except the shrill sound of our moms calling us in for dinner as the sun went down. Our two-wheelers toted us virtually anywhere we wanted to go. They gave us our first taste of real freedom. On our bikes, we would cut swaths through new terrain, snaking in and out of new worlds with bright eyes, wide smiles, and pure hearts. Somewhere along the way, however, we lost interest. We grew up, and bikes gave way to cars. We pushed our bicycles to the periphery: to the corners of our garages and out of our minds. That was the point at which we began to lose sight of the pure, unadulterated joy of exercise.

Now is the time to rekindle your love of cycling, to shine it up, to get back on—and to ride fast.

The bicycle is arguably the most miraculous machine ever invented. It converts the power of your legs into forward motion with fantastic efficiency. In this book, I am going to teach you to ride your bike better and stronger than you ever have in your life. This isn't merely about getting into "decent shape" again; you owe yourself more than that. This is about tapping into the thrilling feeling of *riding fast*: 0 to 25 miles an hour in 10 weeks. That's my promise to you.

This quest is not merely about performance, however. You will tap into the passion you felt for the bike as a child. You will remember how to pedal with bright eyes, a wide smile, and a pure heart. Approaching your cycling this way will make the journey more satisfying, and it will help make exercise a rewarding and permanent part of your life. We want these 10 weeks to catalyze a love affair with exercise that lasts a lifetime.

Having a quantifiable, performance-oriented goal—in this case striving to ride 25 miles per hour—will help to motivate and inspire you in a positive way. It will force you outside of your comfort zone and push your limits. The best part about focusing on *performance* is that if you have weight-loss goals, you will rocket by them so fast on your way to 25 miles per hour that you won't even realize you hit them. It's a whole lot easier than "grinding it out" to lose 10 pounds.

Your "strive for 25" requires that you recruit the power of your mind as much as your body. In the next several chapters, I will outline 25 clear, action-oriented strategies that will get you moving at 25 miles an hour.

Each one of the strategies—whether it has to do with how to eat before workouts, how to pedal fluidly through 360 degrees, or how to climb, descend, and corner better—will directly translate to 1 mile per hour on the road. Success comes from small, manageable steps.

This book is about your momentum: getting moving, gathering steam, and staying in motion for the rest of your life.

Whatever your current state of fitness, you can regain your momentum—and the bicycle is the right apparatus to help you do that. The physics of cycling are favorable to the push-and-pull forces of momentum. It's easy to get rolling on a bike, and once you're going, the bike does much of the work to keep you in motion.

There's no better time to begin riding your bicycle than right now. So come on, saddle up. Let's roll.

I've found that the easiest way to reach a fitness-related goal is to do three things.

1. Do what you love. (If you picked up this book, then you love cycling.)

2. Follow an incredibly fun—but also scientifically grounded—training program.

3. Push yourself past what you thought was possible.

Those are the three principles of this book. That is why I've decided to set a goal for you of 25 miles an hour. It may sound like an arbitrary goal, but here's my reasoning: By shooting for a performance-based goal, in this case a 3-mile time trial at 25 miles an hour, you are able to stay focused on the objective while honing your skills and stoking that fire in your belly.

I'm laying out a 10-week program in which you ride anywhere from 3 to 6 days a week; that depends on you, your current fitness level, and your goals. I ask that you dedicate at least 4 hours a week to this program. I also ask that you not ride any more than 10 hours a week. Why? Because after that, it's seriously diminishing returns. Riding better is not a matter of putting in a lot of hours; it's a matter of your putting a lot *into* those hours. Quality over quantity. And above all else, this has to be fun. No matter how serious you are about riding fast, you need to make fun the focus. That way, the destination will come and the journey will have been enjoyed.

1

PLAN OVERVIEW

All you need to get rolling on this program is a bicycle in good working order, a helmet, shoes, and a couple of basic cycling outfits. While proper gear will help you ride faster and more enjoyably, your head, heart, and lungs will propel you more than any slick gear or aluminum bike, so don't overspend on the accoutrements!

Your Basic Gear Checklist

Since you already ride, you likely have a lot of these items, but it's helpful to go over a complete checklist just to make sure you have everything in order.

• *Bicycle.* You don't need one of those space-age bikes to achieve your goal of riding 25 miles an hour; the bike's fit and your fitness determine your success more than anything you can buy. I'll provide you with some great tips on getting fitted properly on your bike a little bit later. As to the components of your bicycle, it's best to go with what is comfortable and durable. For example, if you prefer handlebars with drops because you like the feeling of getting low and

splitting the wind, then by all means go with drops. However, if you prefer a more upright posture on the bike, then you can use another handlebar configuration. When it comes to cycling, what matters most is what's in your heart, not what's under your body!

That said, get a bike that is durable and comfortable. I suggest you ride a half-dozen road bikes at your local shop and research your favorites in magazines or online at www.roadbikereview.com. What-

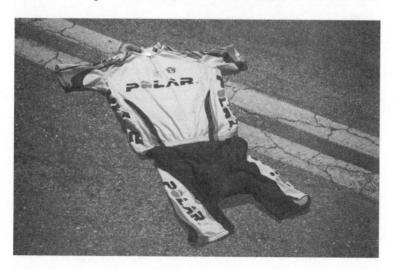

ever you do, don't spend a dime over $1,000 for your new bike. The return on your money precipitously declines once you've passed that threshold.

• *Clothing.* Cycling-specific shorts include padding designed to eliminate chafing and rubbing on sensitive areas, so don't scrimp on quality here. Besides being less comfortable, a cheap pair will begin to wear after a couple of months, rendering your backside exposed to people behind you. A cycling top should be light, tight, and made of a fabric that wicks the moisture away from your body. Bike gloves reduce road shock and protect you, as in the event of a crash, when you instinctively put your hands down first. Invest in three pairs of shorts, three tops, and a couple of pairs of gloves. Being able to rotate all of this gear is nice when yesterday's outfit is at the bottom of the laundry pile! Expect to spend between $300 and $400 on all of this clothing.

• *Shoes.* You have two choices: running shoes with toe-clip pedals or clipless cycling shoes. If you are aiming to ride at 25 miles an hour, you must go clipless. This is nonnegotiable—you will cycle with a great deal more power and fluidity, and it's easier to clip out, or exit, from the pedals. Have an experienced bicycle expert set your cleats to ensure the safest and best path for your knees during the

pedal stroke. This limits the stress on your knees, joints, and back. The cost of cycling shoes? $80 to $120.

• *Helmet.* Another nonnegotiable item. A helmet may save your life, and you should wear it during all training rides, period. Your helmet should sit level on your head and should line up with the middle of your forehead, and the straps should be snug. If you're able to move the helmet backward or forward so that the back or front of your

head is exposed, then the helmet is too loose. Even if you're going for a spin around the block, put it on. Expect to spend $60 on a high-quality helmet. Spend less and sacrifice safety—and fashion! The supercheap models more closely resemble a large Styrofoam beer cooler than a bicycle helmet!

• *Sunglasses.* A good pair of shades is less about fashion and more about function. Sunglasses will protect your eyes from the sun, wind, and other elements (such as insects hurtling at your eyes at 25 miles an hour). Ouch!

• *Heart rate monitor.* This is the most important training tool you can buy. The program in this book requires that you work out based on percentages of your maximum heart rate in order to get the most possible benefit from your riding time. For recreational cyclists, get a Polar M61 heart rate monitor ($150). For you more serious riders out there, a Polar S720i is an all-in-one cyclecomputer and heart rate monitor. This provides the highest level of personal performance data and includes training conditions like altitude and temperature, plus all cycling functions. Infrared technology allows you to download directly to your PC without a separate interface! You'll spend $300 for this model, but if you're serious about cycling, it's well worth the investment.

• *Rearview mirror.* Obviously, this allows you to see behind you at all times. It works just like the one in your car, heightens your awareness of everything around you, and costs only $10.

Practice "Heads-Up" Riding

Here are some tips for riding smart and safe.

Stay loose. Focus on relaxing your entire body when you ride. Some people tend to tense up, particularly when riding faster or in windy weather. By staying loose, you will ride faster and more efficiently.

Stay alert. As you grow stronger on the bike, you'll find that the road will "roll up" on you more quickly. By that I mean you'll cover more ground more quickly! Be vigilant in scanning the road well ahead of you for hazards, and remain aware of cars, pedestrians, and other cyclists.

Stay balanced. Keep your weight well centered on the bike, whether you're taking a corner or climbing up hills.

Stay smart. Use good judgment when riding near cars or pedestrians. Expect them to do the unexpected. Anticipate sudden moves. Use your head, and you'll be less likely to fall on it!

Stay smooth. Pedal in nice, smooth circles. Don't mash down on the pedals. "Kick across" the top of the stroke and sweep your foot through the bottom of the stroke.

Stay cool. Never lose your temper at a driver, cyclist, or pedestrian. It's a no-win situation—at best, you'll feel vindicated (and look like a jerk). At worst,

you could find yourself in a dangerous situation. If someone does something stupid and almost knocks you off your bike, you can either ask them to be more careful next time or simply move on.

Training Plan Overview: Your Road Map

Now it's time to design your cycling "road map." To achieve the lofty goal of riding a bicycle at 25 miles an hour, you need a well-conceived, efficient, and easy-to-follow plan. If you were going to build a home, you wouldn't begin the project without expertly crafted blueprints, would you? Yet it's surprising how many people seek to build their bodies without the right plan to go about doing it.

Rather than bog you down with a litany of exercise dos and don'ts and mind-numbing workouts, we're going to do things differently here. Over the next 10 weeks, you will focus on three key workouts each week. That's it. When you do them is up to you. However, I ask three things.

1. You must do each of them *every week.*

2. You must do them *correctly.*

3. You must fully rest before and fully recover from these workouts. The amount of rest you need to be "fully rested" varies from person to person. Basically, you should feel physically "fresh" and raring to go, and mentally you should feel motivated. Those are two good indications that you are prepared for a key workout. As for the recovery part of the equation, after a key workout, you should not train strenuously again until your muscle soreness and fatigue have all but disappeared. This normally takes 2 to 5 days, depending on the duration and intensity of the workout.

I want to protect you from the mistakes of overtraining or hitting plateaus, so I need to dispel a common exercise myth. The "no pain, no gain" or "harder is better" approach is prevalent and potentially hazardous. When it comes to your body, harder is not better—*smarter* is better. Studies have shown that the body responds best to exercise when you conduct both hard and easy workouts, in the right balance, throughout the week.

The Borg rating of perceived exertion, or RPE, scale provides a quantitative measure of exercise effort. To determine your RPE, do a brief mental scan of your body while working out. How labored is your breathing? How hard are your muscles working? Then use the following scale to give your "exercise effort" a number.

RPE Scale

0 to 7: Very, very light exertion. (This is a feeling similar to that of getting up from the couch to get a beer. Needless to say, you'll have to push harder than an RPE of 7 if you want to get back into great shape!)

8 to 9: Very light exertion. (You barely feel like you're exercising.)

10 to 11: Fairly light exertion. (You're just starting to break a sweat.)

12 to 14: Somewhat hard exertion. (Your breathing is becoming fairly labored.)

15: Hard exertion. (You feel the beginnings of a lactic acid sensation in your muscles. That's the familiar "burning" feeling you get as you increase the intensity of a workout.)

16 to 17: Very hard exertion. (You cannot speak one sentence without running out of breath. Rivulets of drool may begin to appear.)

18 to 19: Very, very hard exertion. (You cannot speak.)

20: Maximum exertion.

In your cycling program over the next 10 weeks, you'll break down your workouts into three simple levels of exercise intensity. RPE will be one of your methods for gauging your intensity level.

Level I: Recovery/Endurance/Anatomical Adaptation

Duration: 20 minutes to 2+ hours.

Subjective Effort Level: Nice, steady pace. A Level I workout should be performed at a pace that you could conceivably sustain for 4 hours, though clearly you won't go for that long.

RPE: 10 to 12.

Objective Effort Level: 50 to 60 percent of maximum heart rate. Generally, at this level, your heart rate should not exceed 140 beats per minute. Your longer rides build your mental and physical endurance.

Benefits: This level enhances aerobic fitness, and fat is the primary fuel source.

Level II: Long "Cruise" Intervals

Duration: 2 to 8 minutes each.

Subjective Effort Level: These workouts feel "comfortably challenging." You're working fairly hard, but you're under control.

RPE: 12 to 14.

Objective Effort Level: 60 to 75 percent of maximum heart rate.

Benefits: These sessions prepare you to ride at a steady, sustained pace. The goal of your tempo rides, those at a "moderately hard, sustained pace," is to build up to 3 miles at an average speed of 25 miles an hour. For example, in week 3, after a thorough warmup, you might ride for 2 minutes at 25 miles per hour. Then, in week 4, you increase that to 3 minutes. With that kind of steady, easy progression, at the end of 10 weeks, you'll have arrived at that 7½-minute goal!

Level III: Short Intervals/Speed

Duration: 30 seconds to 2 minutes each.

Subjective Effort Level: Hard.

RPE: 14 to 16.

Objective Effort Level: 70 to 80 percent of maximum heart rate.

Benefits: These workouts will help you break through fitness "plateaus" by challenging your body to work well outside of your comfort zone. (*Important note:* Level III workouts should be performed only after at least 4 weeks of consistent, injury-free exercise.) These sessions help you get into tremendous mental and physical shape by pushing your limits. Your cycling goal is 25 miles an hour. If you can perform a few 1-minute efforts at 28 to 30 miles an hour, "coming back" to 25 miles an hour will feel appreciably easier.

Different levels of effort produce different results in your body. For example, if you want to lose body fat or increase your endurance, longer workouts at a milder intensity (Level I workouts) will produce the best results. If you want to be a competitive athlete, then you should include more tempo (Level II) sessions. They teach your body to sustain higher power outputs over time. Therefore, it's important to vary your exercise intensity constantly throughout the week so that you can enjoy steady progress with a minimum amount of fatigue.

It's important that you understand the design principles at work in your training program. These are the principles of any good exercise plan. So, remember to follow these three simple rules.

1. Rest days should fall 2 days before and the day after key workouts. This allows your body to be better prepared for your most important sessions and to recover from them as well.

2. Your long ride should fall on a Saturday or Sunday, or when you normally have the most free time.

3. Mondays are ideal off days, because it's nice not to have to worry about working out in addition to the mental stress of heading back to the office!

Strengthen Your Body in Five Simple Moves

By strengthening your body using weight-training exercises, you will build the stamina, resilience, and power to reach your true potential on the bike. You'll perform at a higher level during your cycling workouts and recover more quickly from rides. You'll also be able to perform all of your day-to-day functions more efficiently and with less pain.

The great essayist and orator Philip Dormer Stanhope might not have been a fitness buff, but he understood the importance of stretching, saying, "Prepare yourself for the world, as the athletes . . . do for their exercise; oil your mind and your manners, to give them the necessary suppleness and flexibility; strength alone will not do."

Here's why stretching is an important adjunct to strengthening: When you lift weights, your muscles tend to shorten and become a little less flexible. By stretching and strengthening the muscle together, you build a stronger physique that remains supple and loose.

Each of the weight exercises is followed by a related stretch. This is a good way to structure a workout, because when you strengthen a certain body part—say, your upper back—the act of lifting the weight warms the muscles. That provides a perfect opportunity to then stretch the area, since it's best to stretch your muscles when they are warm and more elastic.

The question is, how do you get the most bang for your buck? You needn't do an array of exercises that address every body part. A warm-up, five simple strength moves, and five stretches will confer the maximum benefit in the shortest time, so that you can be in and out of the gym in 40 minutes or less. You'll do the following workout twice a week, on Wednesday and Friday, in weeks 3 through 10 of your training program.

The Warmup

This often gets short shrift, but it's an essential part of your workout, setting the tone for your entire exercise session. "Doing light activity raises your body temperature and literally warms your muscles, making them more flexible and resilient," says Todd Weitzenberg, MD, a sports medicine specialist at Kaiser Permanente in Santa Rosa, California. "This increases your range of motion and boosts your performance. In addition, nerve messages travel faster at higher temperatures, speeding muscle reactions and reflexes and thereby reducing risk of injury."

By starting out slowly with a proper warmup, you ensure that your muscles are well oxygenated before you call on them to do strenuous work. Because oxygen is an ingredient necessary for your body to produce energy, your muscles will function more effectively and powerfully when they're well oxygenated. Do an aerobic activity such as walking on a treadmill or pedaling a stationary bike at a slow, easy pace for 5 minutes. At the end of your warmup, you should just be breaking a sweat. If you start to get a bit winded, you're going too hard.

The Workout

Use a weight that significantly challenges you in the last few repetitions of each set of dumbbell exercises. You might start with 10-pound dumbbells and increase the weight as you grow stronger.

.

THE LUNGE

This move develops every major muscle group of the lower body in a way that slightly mimics the motion of pedaling a bike. It strengthens the entire leg and butt while increasing the range of motion in the hips, making it a dynamite exercise for cycling.

1. Stand holding two dumbbells at your sides, your feet shoulder-width apart and your toes pointing straight ahead.

2. Take a big stride forward, far enough so that your front thigh ends up parallel to the floor with your knee over (but not past) your toes. Push back up to the starting position by bringing your front leg to your back leg. Do a set of 12 repetitions with each leg. Rest for 30 seconds after your first set, and during that time do the quadriceps stretch on the opposite page. (Your quads are the four muscles on the front of your thigh.) Then do a second set of lunges with each leg, this time of 8 repetitions. End the sequence by stretching your quads for about 1 minute before moving on to the next exercise.

QUADRICEPS STRETCH

Okay. Are you ready for a killer quad stretch? Stand with your feet shoulder-width apart. Grab your right foot with your right hand, giving it a nice, steady pull while breathing out. Hold the stretch for 2 to 4 seconds. Repeat the stretch with your left foot. Alternate sides for 5 to 6 repetitions.

ONE-ARM ROW

This develops all the muscles in your upper back and simulates the motion of pulling on the handlebars when you're out of the saddle on the bike.

1. Holding a dumbbell in your right hand, place your left hand and knee on a workout bench or an exercise ball. Keep your back flat, and let the dumbbell hang down at your side so that it's directly below your shoulder.

2. Focus on using your upper-back muscles as you pull the dumbbell up and back toward your shoulder, keeping your arm close to your body. Pause at the top of the move, and then slowly lower the dumbbell to the starting position. Do 12 reps with your right arm and 12 with your left. Follow the set with the upper-back stretch on the opposite page.

UPPER-BACK STRETCH

Here's a great upper-back stretch. Stand about 2 feet from a wall and place your hands on the wall roughly 1 foot above your head and 1 foot apart. Then "lean" into the wall and look down at the floor. Breathe into the stretch and really visualize those muscles of your upper back loosening up and elongating. Hold the stretch for 2 to 4 seconds, and repeat it 5 to 6 times. Once you've completed that, do a set of 8 reps with each arm, and stretch the upper-back muscles once again.

STABILITY BALL LEG CURL

This strengthens your hamstrings (the muscle group on the back of your thigh), butt, and "core" (abs and lower back) and develops balance and coordination. You'll need a stability ball for this exercise. These large, inflatable plastic balls develop many muscles concurrently because of the balancing involved and are available at most gyms. They cost about $20.

1. Lie on your back on a carpeted floor or an exercise mat with your legs extended and your heels up on a stability ball. Keep your arms folded behind your head or straight out at your sides with your palms down—whichever position is more comfortable. Press down through your heels on the ball to lift your pelvis, butt, and most of your back off the floor. Your body should form a bridge from your shoulder blades to your feet, and you should feel the exertion in the muscles along the backs of your thighs and in your midsection.

2. Keeping your body lifted, squeeze your gluteal muscles, and press your feet flat into the ball as you bend your knees and roll the ball in toward you, pause, and then roll the ball back out to the bridge position. Roll the ball in and out 12 times before doing the hamstring stretch on the opposite page for 30 seconds.

HAMSTRING STRETCH

One great way to stretch your hamstrings is to lie on your back with your legs bent so that your feet are flat on the floor. Use a rope or towel to pull one foot up until you feel a nice, gentle stretch right in the middle of your hamstrings. Hold the stretch for 2 to 4 seconds. Now do the same with the opposite leg. Continue to stretch, alternating legs, for 5 to 6 repetitions.

CHEST FLY

This is the best exercise for your chest and arms, because it concurrently strengthens all of the muscles of the chest as well as your biceps, forearms, and triceps. Although it's your legs that power the forward motion in cycling, it's important to have a strong upper body, too. That's because when you're climbing out of the saddle, for example, you're constantly pulling on the handlebars and using your upper body to balance yourself. When you're riding fast, cornering, or descending, you also need a strong upper body to remain stable and balanced on your bike.

1. Grasp the dumbbells and lie on your back on the floor, a bench, or an exercise ball. Beginning with the dumbbells together "at the top," slowly lower them to your chest. If you can move them a little past your chest, that is ideal. Once you reach the bottom, hold them there for half a second, and then push them back up to the starting position.

2. Use your chest muscles to squeeze the dumbbells together in front of your chest. Pause before returning to the starting position. Do 12 repetitions, and then take a 30-second rest (use the rest time to do the chest stretch on the opposite page). Do another set of 8 repetitions, followed by the chest stretch for 1 minute.

CHEST STRETCH

To stretch your chest, clasp both hands behind you and press your chest forward.

CRUNCH

This exercise strengthens your core without subjecting you to painful or awkward contraptions.

1. Lie on your back with your knees bent and your feet flat on the floor about hip-width apart. Place your hands lightly behind your head to gently support it.

2. Use your abs to lift your head and shoulder blades 4 to 6 inches off the floor. Keep your lower back pressed firmly against the floor and your elbows pointing straight out (not forward). Hold a tight crunch for 10 to 15 seconds as you exhale, and then slowly lower yourself back to the starting position. Rest for 15 seconds, and repeat 10 times. Then perform one of the abs stretches on the opposite page.

ABS STRETCHES

Do one of the following stretches for 1 minute.

For the ball drape stretch, drape yourself over a stability ball faceup, and allow your entire body to relax deeply into the stretch.

To perform a cobra yoga stretch, lie facedown and push your upper body up while keeping your pelvis on the floor. Keep your arms straight and your hands facing forward.

Advanced Skill: SuperSlow

Resistance training is a scientifically proven way to increase strength and muscle tone, rev up metabolism, improve endurance, boost stamina, and prevent pain and injury by fortifying ligaments and tendons and strengthening bones. It is one of the best things you can do to improve your cycling. But with all the iterations of resistance training out there—Dyna-Bands, flexibands, dumbbells, Nautilus machines, high repetitions, low repetitions—what is the best way to do it?

Some experts believe that if you want a stronger, leaner, more resilient physique, you'll get there faster by slowing things down. "By moving weights at a very slow pace, you eliminate any momentum that might help get the weights up faster and make it easier on the muscle," says Fredrick Hahn, author of *The Slow Burn Fitness Revolution: The Slow Motion Exercise That Will Change Your Body in 30 Minutes a Week*.

A new form of resistance training is known as SuperSlow. Super-Slow training originated in 1982 from a 5-year osteoporosis program at the University of Florida Medical School. Working with an older group of individuals, the researchers sought to devise a safer and more effective way of loading and exercising muscles. The result was a new form of strength training, later deemed SuperSlow.

The primary objective of SuperSlow resistance training is to create more tension in a muscle while lifting the weight, simply by slowing the speed of movement. Physiologically, lifting more slowly and deliberately activates a greater number of muscle fibers for a given movement. That provides more strength development in a shorter period of time.

Some experts believe that SuperSlow resistance training is superior to traditional strength training in three important ways:

1. It's safer. Moving more slowly reduces the amount of ballistic force, or high-speed/impact stress, on the body, which reduces the risk of pain or injury.

2. Lifting a weight more slowly reduces momentum, and since momentum essentially unloads the muscle you are trying to load, moving more slowly provides more focused benefit to the muscle.

3. To gain maximum benefit from strength training, you must fully isolate the muscle you are working on. Many people tend to cheat a movement

in the weight room by twisting, arching their backs, or slightly bending their knees to lift a weight. By moving more slowly, you tend to better focus—mentally and physically—on the working muscle, which confers more benefit.

In his book *SuperSlow: The Ultimate Exercise Protocol,* Ken Hutchins says, "In a nutshell, SuperSlow is raising the weight in 10 seconds and lowering the weight in 10 seconds. There are minor exceptions to this, but this is the basic plan. If you perform an arm-bending movement and time yourself, you will see that this is creepy slow."

In SuperSlow weight training, you complete 4 to 6 repetitions, rather than the traditional 12 to 15. If you are currently engaged in a strength-training program, you'll likely need to reduce the weight of your exercises by 30 to 40 percent to handle the increased load associated with slower, 20-second lifts. "Two intense 20-minute sessions per week will provide optimal results," says Hutchins. "And keep each SuperSlow workout more than 2 days apart to let the muscles repair and recover fully," he says.

When you perform this motion, the key is to keep the movements and the turnarounds (at the top and bottom of the motion) as fluid and smooth as possible. This more fully isolates the muscle and reduces stress on the body. Be sure to breathe deeply through the entire movement.

A potential disadvantage of this training is that because you are moving the weight more slowly, your muscles are under load for longer periods of time—and that can feel a little more strenuous than regular weight training. But SuperSlow embodies the "quality over quantity" exercise maxim. While this new way of strength training may be a little more intense, you'll reap more benefit from it in a much shorter period of time. And believe me; you will feel the results on the bike.

I've been engaging in SuperSlow training for the past 6 weeks, and in that time I've developed a strength that seems to run to every fiber of my body. This form of resistance training has made me faster, stronger, and more resilient than any I've tried. If you've experienced a plateau in your riding, or if you just want to explore a new, exciting form of re-shaping your body, give SuperSlow a go—and see how it makes you look, feel, . . . and ride!

To learn more about SuperSlow training, visit www.superslow.com.

NUTRITION

There are so many fad diets out there, and these days it's all but impossible to know what, when, or *how* to eat! But rest assured—you needn't alter your diet too much on this program. Over the weeks, just try to integrate these four strategies into your diet.

When Making Food Choices, Use the Glycemic Index

I learned the term *slow food* in Vernazza, a small Italian village in the Cinque Terre region. The waiter asked if I preferred his slow food to our American fast food. I most certainly did. While I was in Italy, my energy felt steadier, I enjoyed eating more, because I was indulging in lots of delicious foods—including ice cream—and amazingly, I was *losing* some body fat.

The Italians eat more fat than we do, they enjoy their food more, and somehow they're in better shape than we are. Here in America, we've never eaten less fat; eating has become a stressful, ambivalent act; and we've never been fatter. We're getting a raw deal!

In terms of macronutrient composition (fats, carbohydrates, and proteins), the Mediterranean diet is more balanced than ours. That's because it includes more high-quality fats such as those in olive oil and fresh fish. These foods elicit slower blood sugar responses and steadier insulin levels, which translate into less stored body fat and healthier hearts.

To understand why the Mediterranean diet is more balanced (and possibly healthier) than ours, we need look no further than a food rating system called the glycemic index (GI) of foods. The GI was introduced in the early 1980s to tabulate the effects of foods on blood sugar. This is important to you because your blood sugar levels directly influence your energy level and, to a lesser extent, the size of your belly.

The GI ranks foods on measured blood sugar levels compared with that of pure glucose, which is rated 100. Foods are grouped into those with a high GI (scores from 70 to 100, such as bread and breakfast cereal), a moderate GI (40 to 70, such as oatmeal and dairy foods), or a low GI (10 to 40, including nuts, meats, and cold-climate fruits such as apples).

When you drink a soda with a GI of roughly 40, for example, it sends your blood sugar skyward, which gives you an initial burst of energy. To remove that excess blood sugar, your pancreas releases insulin—almost invariably, excess insulin, removing too much blood sugar. That's why you get that energy crash roughly 20 minutes after eating a high-carbohydrate or high-sugar snack. But there's more bad news: Some studies show that when there are large amounts of insulin in your body, body fat is metabolized less efficiently. So when you have something high in sugar or carbohydrates, such as a fruit smoothie or bagel, before your workout, you may burn less body fat.

Many Americans have chronically elevated insulin levels, because carbohydrates are ubiquitous and so easy to eat. In addition, our meals are culturally prescribed: We have coffee, juice, and a Danish for breakfast; a sandwich, chips, and a soda for lunch; and pasta for dinner. All of these foods are very high on the glycemic index. Translation? A fatter you.

You've probably heard of the Atkins diet, or some iteration of that diet, by now. Simply put, Atkins instructs people to eat foods low on the glycemic index by eschewing carbs and sugar for proteins and fats. It's that simple. In my opinion, this isn't the best way to eat, but integrating the principles of Atkins helps to balance people's diets, which are normally too high in carbohydrates and sugars.

The glycemic index is a useful tool in managing your weight, because low-GI foods have been shown to produce a longer-lasting satiated feeling after meals, which translates into fewer total calories eaten. Don't take my word for it: How do you feel after a peanut butter sandwich? It keeps you satisfied for a longer period of time, and in the final analysis, you end up eating fewer total calories.

The trick is to graze on lower glycemic index foods, namely high-quality fats and proteins. Don't be afraid to eat like the French—snack on a slice of brie and an apple. This will make you feel better and will stabilize your blood sugar levels, leading to steadier energy and better weight management. This is exactly how many of the world's best athletes eat. (This doesn't mean you can eat five Ho-Hos a day. It's important to distinguish between high-quality fats, such as that in olive oil, and bad fats, such as hydrogenated oils, which are commonly found in cookies, cakes, and sweets.)

An Ideal Day of Eating

Here is an ideal day of eating following the principles of the glycemic index, along with approximate GI scores. (Remember: Grazing on smaller meals is healthier than eating fewer but larger meals.)

Breakfast (7 a.m.): Two eggs, with one yolk removed (GI = 49), or oatmeal with butter (41); hot cocoa or tea (53). (No fruit juice—it is very high on the GI.)

Snack (10 a.m.): One large apple and a spoonful of peanut butter (41).

Lunch (12 p.m.): One-half turkey sandwich on whole-grain bread (61).

Snack (3:30 p.m.): The other half of that sandwich.

Pre-exercise (4 p.m.): Protein shake (31).

Postexercise (7 p.m.): Sports drink (88) and bagel (79). (It's beneficial to eat foods higher on the glycemic index after exercise, because your body needs the sugar. If you must have that Snickers, have it post-workout.)

Dinner (7:30 p.m.): Medium-size salad with chicken, beans, and extra-virgin olive oil (48); broccoli (35). Oh, and don't forget that Ben & Jerry's! It's lower on the glycemic index than you may think (52) because of the fats in there. It's also good for the soul! That's what food should be: It should feed more than just your body. So dig into that ice cream, and relish every bite.

For more information on the glycemic index, with specific foods and their corresponding glycemic index numbers, please refer to Appendix B.

Eat Right before and after Workouts

Now that you understand how the glycemic index works, you can make better choices before and after your bike rides.

Preworkout Nutrition

Many people are confused about what to eat before exercise. Should you eat a smoothie? A bagel? An energy bar? You want to feel energized going into a workout so you can get the most benefit out of your hard work, but you don't want your energy to plummet 20 minutes into the bike ride, either. I've found that the best strategy is to have a lower-GI snack 1 to 2 hours before working out. This allows you to start your workout with enough glucose in your bloodstream to get you going and keep you moving without feeling weak or shaky. The snack should be 200 to 400 calories, depending on your daily calorie intake, and should provide a nice balance of carbohydrates, protein, and fat. Some ideal snacks that fill the bill are a peanut butter sandwich, a bagel with cream cheese, or a fruit smoothie, with a scoop of protein powder and a tablespoon of oil added to lower the GI score. The high-quality fats and proteins will give you a longer, more sustained burn during your bike rides.

Postworkout Nutrition

Right after working out, drink at least 2 cups of water, which replenishes the most important substance in your body. Then go ahead and eat a high-carbohydrate snack to replace the glycogen stores you likely used up during your exercise. All you really need is a bagel or a cup of fruit juice within a half hour of finishing.

Drink More Water

Because you will be riding more, you must focus on taking in more clean water. You'd be surprised how much even a little dehydration can contribute to a sense of fatigue. Dehydration actually makes it harder for your blood to deliver oxygen to your muscles and can make your arms and legs feel heavy.

The general rule of thumb is to drink *before* you feel thirsty, because you can lose up to 2 percent of your body weight as sweat or urine before your thirst mechanism sets in. If you tend to sweat a lot during your bike rides, you may need 10 to 20 glasses (8 ounces each) of fluid a day.

Here's a simple four-step fluid schedule to help you stay properly hydrated.

1. Two hours before you exercise, drink 3 cups of fluid.

2. Ten to 15 minutes before you exercise, drink 2 cups.

3. Every 15 minutes during exercise, drink 1 cup.

4. After exercise, drink 2 cups.

You can also weigh yourself before and after a workout or race to see how much fluid you've lost and how much you need to replenish. One pound of body weight equals roughly 2 cups (500 milliliters) of fluid.

"Does all that fluid have to be water?" you might ask. Actually, no— there are some wonderful new enhanced fluid beverages out there now, like SoBe. SoBe makes a wide variety of tasty beverages that are enhanced with ingredients such as antioxidants, L-carnitine, and taurine. My philosophy has always been that if something tastes good, you'll drink more of it . . . as long as it's healthy! Fortified drinks like SoBe also contain small amounts of sodium and potassium, two minerals lost when you sweat, so they are a better choice than empty sugar drinks. But if you routinely drink sports drinks instead of water, the calories can

(Continued on page 34)

The Seven Best Foods for Longevity

To boost your health and your cycling performance, it may be more helpful to focus on what you *should* eat rather than on what you shouldn't. The National Institutes of Health recently reported that type 2 diabetes, a debilitating disease, afflicts more than 16 million Americans. And that number is on the rise, due in large part to how we eat.

"Too many calories devoid of nutritional value, too little exercise, and obesity are the key risk factors for this dreadful condition," says Elaine Gavalas, PhD, an exercise physiologist, a nutritionist, and a contributing author of *Alternative Medicine: The Definitive Guide.*

Dr. Gavalas explains that you can decrease your risk of type 2 diabetes—in addition to preventing heart disease, cancer, obesity, hormonal imbalances, and other illnesses—simply by *adding* more healthy foods to your daily diet rather than depriving yourself of foods you enjoy. You're also likely to drop a few pounds and experience a boost in energy.

While it's nearly impossible to come to a consensus on the healthiest foods, a 1999 study published in the *Journal of the American Medical Association* found that people who ate more of the following foods had a "30 percent lower risk of death from all causes."

Fresh Wild Salmon

Delicious and with exceptional nutritional value found in few other foods, salmon is a bonanza for your health. Each 3½-ounce portion of salmon provides a whopping 20 grams of protein and 6 to 7 grams of very healthy fat—1.2 grams of which are omega-3 fatty acids, which is near the recommended daily intake for adults.

Tip: Choose wild over farmed salmon. It's better for the environment, and it's better for you.

Garlic

Arguably the most powerful disease- and ailment-fighting food on the planet. Studies abound extolling the health virtues of this wonder food, but perhaps garlic's greatest practical value is its antiviral property: It kills viruses responsible for colds and the flu, according to tests by James North, PhD, a microbiologist at Brigham Young University in Provo, Utah. "Eat garlic when you feel a sore throat coming on," he says, "and you may not even get sick." Other studies suggest that garlic revs up immune functioning by stimulating infection-fighting T-cells.

Tip: Buy unpackaged garlic, and press the cloves to be sure they're firm. Choose large bulbs with outer skin that is tight, free of soft spots, and unbroken. Eat it raw to maximize its antibacterial and antiviral effects. And, yes, for you breath-conscious folk out there, garlic supplements, such as Garlique, have been shown to work almost as well as the real thing . . . without damaging your social life!

Green Tea

Researchers from the University of Kansas recently measured the antioxidant content of green tea and found that it is roughly 100 times as effective as vitamin C—and 25 times as good as vitamin E—at protecting cells from damage believed to be linked to cancer, heart disease, and other illnesses.

Tip: Aim for fresh teas. I've found the Sencha loose-leaf variety, found at most health food stores, to be the most potent green tea. It also provides a healthy dose of caffeine—ideal before exercise!

Extra-Virgin Olive Oil

According to Elizabeth Somer, MA, RD, a registered dietitian in Salem, Oregon, olive oil provides a double-whammy boost to your health: "Saturated fats in meat and fatty dairy products raise your 'bad' LDL cholesterol, which tends to clog arteries, and lower your 'good' HDL cholesterol, which tends to clear arteries," she says. "So your goal is to lower LDL and raise HDL. In contrast, the polyunsaturated fats in most vegetable oils, such as corn or soy oil, lower LDL but also lower HDL. Olive oil works its magic by lowering your bad cholesterol without affecting your good cholesterol."

Tip: Store olive oil in a cool, dry place, and buy portions large enough to last you only 1 to 2 months, to prevent spoilage. Spend the extra money to get extra-virgin olive oil; the higher quality makes it well worth it.

Red Grapes

Research has shown time and again that moderate consumption of red wine increases health and longevity because of the powerful antioxidant properties of red grapes.

(Continued)

(Cont.)

Tip: The health-promoting effects of red grapes don't give you license to get sloshed on red wine. Exercise moderation. One glass a day (and no more) will calm your spirit and improve your health. *Salute!*

Whole Grains

A 1999 University of Minnesota study found that eating whole grains can increase longevity, because they contain anticancer agents and stabilize blood sugar and insulin levels.

Tip: The best sources are cereals with at least 5 grams of fiber per serving and multigrain breads such as pumpernickel, rye, or whole wheat.

Clean Water

While water isn't a food, of course, it is one of the most important ingredients to good health. But you must choose wisely. "Because the disinfecting process can eliminate many valuable minerals in bottled water, the water's source is critical," says Arthur von Wiesenberger, generally regarded as one of the world's leading experts on water. "A deep, protected, and monitored source is important because it guarantees purity and minimizes the need for disinfecting."

Tip: The bottled water industry is by and large unregulated—many of

really start to add up. I'd stick to no more than 16 ounces of sports drinks a day, even on heavy training days, and get most of your fluids from water.

Tip: A good strategy is to take a stand at the grocery store. In other words, don't let the bad stuff make it past your front door—start by keeping it out of your shopping cart! You can achieve that by not shopping on an empty stomach, sticking to a predetermined list, or even heading to cyberspace for your groceries. There are services (such as Safeway.com) that allow you to shop online and have food delivered to your door for a nominal fee. It's easier to shop healthy when it's virtual, because you can't see, feel, and smell those chocolate doughnuts!

these products are little more than slickly packaged tap water. Find out more about the bottled waters that you are drinking.

Ice Cream/Chocolate

I have an incurable addiction to these two foods. I readily admit that. Notwithstanding my weakness, the mental-health properties of comfort foods like these should not be underestimated. Yes, you need to indulge in foods that make you feel good—that's part of living fully! It is why I have included these two foods on the list.

Medical studies have shown that the phenylethylamine found in chocolate clearly boosts one's mood. The Aztecs are documented to have used cocoa as a medicinal ingredient. Even the celebrated French physician Francis Joseph Victor Broussais declared in 1788, "Chocolate of good quality . . . calms the fever, nourishes . . . the patient, and tends to restore him to health."

Eating nutritious foods, such as the ones on this list, while also indulging in foods that make you feel good is a more balanced way to improve your health through nutrition. Just be sure to heed your mom's timeless advice of eating more veggies and whole grains than you do chocolate and ice cream.

Graze

You may have learned from an early age that the best way to get your nutrition is to "get in those three squares a day!" But new research suggests that people who eat six smaller meals a day are healthier and have an easier time maintaining their weight and cholesterol levels. When you eat more than about 600 calories at one sitting, your body stores the rest as body fat. In addition, your blood sugar determines your energy levels. So if you graze every few hours on 200- to 300-calorie, low-sugar, protein-oriented snacks (bagel with cream cheese, turkey sandwich, salad with olive oil, yogurt), your energy will grow and your waistline will shrink.

Get Motivated to Eat Right

The National Institutes of Health recently issued a shocking report: Obesity has surpassed lung disease as the number-one killer in the United States. As a nation, America is spending more money than ever on its collective fitness and weight loss, and we are more awash in nutrition and diet information than ever before. How can it be, then, that Americans are dying at a faster rate than ever from being overweight?

There are many possible answers: the prevalence of junk food in our diet, a lack of reliable nutrition information, or the proliferation of higher-fat, processed foods. Another answer may be that our increasing reliance on other people or products to solve our weight or eating issues may not be as effective as trusting ourselves.

It's time to pursue better nutrition from the inside out rather than the outside in. It's time to turn away from the late-night infomercials, diet fads, and quick-fix solutions, and rely instead on ourselves to eat better. How do you do that?

The first step is to become intrinsically motivated to eat right. Most people will admit that good health is an important priority in their lives and that they need to lose weight, yet they will continue to make poor diet choices. Jay C. Kimiecik, PhD, a professor at Miami University in Oxford, Ohio, and a consultant on exercise programming for a number of health and fitness organizations, offers a good explanation for this paradox. "Most people who are long-term 'maintainers' [of good eating habits] keep at it because they have learned to want to eat well rather than doing it simply because they should," he says. The secret to these maintainers is called "intrinsic motivation." People who want to eat healthier for its own sake rather than for the rewards or outcomes the behavior might produce are bound to perform better in the long run. That doesn't mean it's wrong to want to get healthy, lose weight, or increase longevity through good nutrition—just that the outcomes like these are unlikely to be enough to keep people eating right for a lifetime.

Developing a long-term intrinsic motivation to eat well begins with simply enjoying good food more. Don't think of this in terms of depriving yourself of the foods you love but rather having more fun with healthier foods. For example, prepare good-for-you foods in a more enjoyable way by following more creative and fun recipes. And be sure to eat the naughty foods once in a while, too! The bottom line with nutrition is this: Ignore all the fad diets and just enjoy your food. The best way to eat has and always will be a simple, wholesome, and balanced diet that *makes you feel good.* Use common sense, trust your body and your instincts, and do your best to make good food choices each day.

To learn building blocks of good nutrition, check out the Food and Nutrition Information Center at www.nalusda.gov/fnic.

GETTING STARTED: WEEKS 1 AND 2

The starting point of all achievement is desire. Keep this constantly in mind. Weak desires bring weak results, just as a small amount of fire makes a small amount of heat.

–Napoleon Hill, American motivational author (1883–1970)

This chapter lays out what you need to do in the first 2 weeks to start improving on your bicycle. Indeed, the toughest part of advancing your cycling program is igniting the fire, getting started.

Motivational quicksand: We've all been there. No matter how much you try to stick with an exercise plan, you instead find yourself rearranging your sock drawer for the umpteenth time or getting sucked toward the freezer for an ice cream fix, double scoop. These fits and starts can be frustrating, and if you experience enough of them, you might want to throw in the towel on this whole exercise thing.

The first step is to abandon the all-or-nothing, destination-oriented exercise approach. When most people come back to working out after a long layoff, they view physical fitness as something to be "achieved."

Their goal normally takes the form of a desired weight or performance level, and they will strive doggedly to attain that goal. However, doing too much too soon can lead to pain, injury, and eventually a complete mental meltdown—plunging you back into your vicious cycle of ice cream and couch-potato-dom!

For others, the enormity of the task of getting back into shape can feel so daunting that they can't even muster up the will to get started. For example, you may think that riding 25 miles per hour on your bike is out of reach. I'm here to tell you that it's not. People older, heavier, and busier than you have done it. And you'll do it, too!

The key to approaching any difficult or arduous task is to shift your focus. From now on, view your body as a lifetime work of art and your bike as your instrument. Every pedal stroke improves the piece. Every ride is a brush stroke, a positive move forward in your quest to live a better life. In this program, you're continually adding to the painting; if you're superbusy one week and you can fit in only one workout, you improved your canvas—and your life—by one day. Make sense?

Get on Your Bike and Roll (Motivation Follows Action)

Do you remember the movie *Forrest Gump,* in which the title character, played by Tom Hanks, began running one day? He ran around the block, then to the city limits, and then kept going until he had jogged across the country and back. Forrest was able to run those great distances because he didn't think about it. He just ran and ran and ran.

As you take this first step, be like Forrest. Don't evaluate the assignment. If you do, you'll likely skip it. Just start getting dressed for a bike ride. Don't reflect, don't reason, don't analyze. Put on your outfit. Pull on your shoes. Get your bike. Point it in any direction and go.

Each day is a new opportunity to improve your cycling, your health, and your life, so you can come back to riding anytime. *You* control your body. *You*—not your spouse, your boss, your kids, or your television—make choices that result in the body you do or don't want. While this may be a difficult notion to accept, it's a must if you want to wrest control over your fitness life. There are 24 hours in each day, and you decide how to use them.

You can decide right this very moment to dust off that old bike and pedal away. Even if it's just a spin around the block, this courageous, all-important first ride will set the wheels in motion. Go right now, and revel in the fact that you have overcome the toughest step of getting back into shape: the first one.

When you take this inaugural ride, strive to be a kid out there. Connect with the bike in the same way a child might. Do you remember when you first learned to ride a bike? Do you recall how it felt to balance on two wheels for the first time? Recapture that sense of newness and innocence. Listen to the sound of the tires scrubbing on the pavement. Take delight in the freedom: On a bicycle, you can explore the world under the power of your own legs. That's as pure a physical experience as you can have.

With each pedal stroke, let your doubts and negative mental messages melt away. For example, thoughts such as "I am moving soooo slowly" or "I am so fat—I'm jiggling!" will only take the steam out of your legs. Replace them with "I am rolling. I've got momentum!" or "I am getting *less* jiggly right now!" You'll be amazed at how energizing, how reassuring, the act of riding can be.

Make the Pledge Right Here, Right Now

Well done! With that first ride, you've cleared the biggest hurdle in your drive for 25. You should be congratulated for doing something few people manage to do: get moving. Your body is in motion. Now it's time to get your *mind* behind your quest.

For a moment, picture your passion. Visualize a time when you were immersed in your favorite activity. Perhaps it was a refreshing run on the beach, a lazy drive through the country, or an uplifting hike up a mountain—anything that deeply resonates with you. What sensations does that image evoke? You likely feel energized, excited, even euphoric. That's because it's an activity for which you feel *passion*—a powerful force that can drive you to great heights. "It's your passion that, throughout your life, will be your saving grace," says Barbara DeAngelis, PhD, in her book *Passion*. "It will keep you going after your dreams when everyone advises you to give up."

The crux of achieving any fitness goal rests with passion. If you have a driving desire to achieve something—and a clear and efficient plan to do that—there really is little you cannot do.

Think about the reason you plucked this book off the shelf and decided to take on this intrepid quest. You already ride your bike, but you want to take your cycling to another level. Maybe you want to enter a local bike race and get your competitive juices flowing. Perhaps you already compete and you want to start winning some races! Whatever your reasons, write them down. Give your explanation in rich, colorful detail.

All this is important because if your mind isn't resolutely behind this quest, your body will not follow. You must develop a deep conviction that over the next 10 weeks, you will let nothing deter you. That requires more than committing to a goal. It demands that you set out on a passion-driven mission.

That means that you must be prepared to integrate your workouts into your workweek. Each week, you must schedule specific dates, times, and locations for your rides. Assign them a high priority. Write them into your daily planner. Treat them as serious business appointments, and don't let anyone take that time from you.

And if you follow all these suggestions, you will succeed in your drive for 25.

Play Up the Positives

I also want you to begin a log, or "Success Journal," in which you will record your best rides over the next 10 weeks. Focusing on each small triumph in your cycling will motivate you to keep going and will send your confidence skyward. It will also be fun to look back on your experiences later on.

Your Success Journal can prop you up on days you feel unmotivated and can keep your passion aflame over the long haul. "In fitness, it's the small, measurable steps that matter," says Susan Kleiner, PhD, RD, a

Check with Your Doctor
Before You Begin Serious Training

Before you set out on this new training program, you must get a checkup from your doctor, especially if you are overweight or have a history of physical problems. An exam will take only an hour or so, but it will serve two vital purposes: First, being aware of health problems before you start training can save your life, as it should alert both you and your doctor to the precautions that need to be taken before you start on an ambitious regimen. Second, a physical exam will determine your baseline health (your weight, cholesterol ratios, body-fat percentage, and so on). Then, at the end of the 10-week program, you can get another exam to see in tangible numbers how your health has improved.

sports nutritionist at High Performance Nutrition in Mercer Island, Washington, and the coauthor of *Power Eating and Fitness Log.* "Making progress in our exercise and diet—and tracking that on paper—motivates and inspires us with confidence." Critical caveat: You must write down the right things. Make copies of Appendix C, and use it to keep the following records.

Assess yourself. "Establishing a baseline of fitness allows you to gauge how you're performing and feeling as you go, and over time that increases your exercise motivation," says sports psychologist Linda Bunker, PhD, of Charlottesville, Virginia. "If you don't know where you started, you'll never get to where you're going." So begin your training and diet plan with an assessment of where you are right now. The first time you fill out a Success Journal worksheet, note some important details, such as the results of your physical exam, your weight, your measurements, how your clothes fit, and the duration and intensity of your bike rides. Write down what you're eating and how much water you're drinking, as well—all of the specifics of your starting point.

Track your training. Record the notable details of the day's ride, such as its length, your route, the weather conditions, your average and maximum speeds, and your average heart rate or subjective effort level.

Know your rights. Your Success Journal is a forum for constructive training lessons and positive workout experiences only; it's not a place to beat yourself up. "Focusing on the positives, rather than the negatives, is more motivating and productive in the long run," says Dr. Kleiner. "That will make you feel successful, and you can build on those successes." Keep a daily record of everything you're doing right to bring yourself closer to your goals, whether it's drinking eight glasses of water a day, improving your position on your bike, or opting for a ride instead of a TV rerun. And remember: Each bike ride moves you closer to your goal.

When recording your daily motivation, write down how inspired you felt that day and what did or didn't fuel your motivation. The goal here is to learn what gets you going and write that down so that you can become better at motivating yourself when you're feeling uninspired. As to mental lessons, write down things that make you feel mentally stronger or how you learned a technique on a ride that gave you more grace under pressure (for example, "During a hard climb, when I cleared my head and just focused on my breathing and pedaling, I felt more in control mentally").

Make it personal. Pursue this quest to become a better, faster cyclist from the inside out rather than the outside in. As you write in your journal, tune in to your positive feelings and what's making the experience so special for you. "Research shows that writing down things that deeply motivate you on a personal level keeps you on track," says Dr. Bunker.

Also, customize your Success Journal so that it completely reflects your cycling life—and you as a person. Build it into a thick, rich, inspiring scrapbook, including the entry form for a big bike race or a medal or ribbon that you won—anything that motivates you. Find ways to make your rides and diet your own, perhaps creating a workout tape of your favorite songs or cooking the healthy foods you truly love. Note how these things are specifically about you and how they make you feel.

"Writing in your journal should be a seamless part of your day," says Dr. Bunker. Keep your journal in a convenient place, and spend a few minutes after every ride writing down your successes, or do it at the end of the day, before bed, just after doing a mental review of all your rights. Pick a time when you'll be most relaxed and excited about recording your victories. You should look forward to tracking and celebrating everything that's going well in your cycling life, so get fired up! Just like riding and eating, this should be fun, cathartic, and passion driven— never guilt inducing. Reviewing each Success Journal entry whenever your motivation wanes will help you get right back on track.

The First 2 Weeks of Your Program

The training program in this book will be workout specific but not training week specific. By that, I mean I will ask that you do a certain number of specific workouts each week, but when you do those workouts will be entirely up to you. I'll make suggestions on when they should occur, but you have a certain weekly routine—with work, family, and social commitments—and you need to be able to shuffle workouts to blend seamlessly into your daily life. Bottom line: You can do the workouts whenever you want each week; just be sure to do them!

In the first 2 weeks of training, the workouts are going to be simple in order to give your body a chance to ease into the program. This will help prevent burnout and injury by strengthening your muscles, ligaments, and tendons more gradually. I know you're excited to ride hard, but trust me: Sure-and-steady progression is the route to go. There will be plenty of time to burn up the pavement later on!

What follows is a specific but simple outline for the first 14 days of your training plan. As you progress, your program will change. I will lay out your program for weeks 3 through 10 in the next chapter; that will have more details, such as heart rate zones, suggested terrain, and so on. For now, as you'll see, the only workouts you'll do are at intensity levels I and II. I am also not going to introduce strength work until week 3, because that is very stressful on the body. Consider these first 2 weeks as a period in which you're transitioning, or "training to train."

Key workouts are in bold italics.

Remember that key workouts are either *longer* or *more intense* than your body is accustomed to. You must be rested before and allow time to recover after these workouts. You must also be alert and engaged, both physically and mentally, during these sessions. That is why you should perform them at the time of day when you feel at your peak. If you're a morning person, get your key workout done early. If you function better in the evening, do the ride after work.

Week 1

Monday: Rest. I can already hear you saying, "Oh, come on. Harr! You're starting me out with a rest day? I picked up your book to get moving!" But you must understand that rest is integral to your overall success on this program. The purpose of rest days is twofold: First, they provide an essential mental and emotional break from training that is absolutely critical to long-term progression. On your rest days, do no stressful exercise. Sure, you can take an easy swim or go for a walk, but do not physically stress your body, even if you're feeling great. You want to harness that energy and unleash it during your key workouts. Remember, those are the sessions that make you stronger, better, faster! Hot baths, massages, and naps are good things to include on your rest days. They also speed up the recovery process by increasing bloodflow and relaxing your muscles.

Tuesday: Level I for 10 to 20 minutes at RPE 11. This is a nice, relaxing ride. Focus on breathing deeply and enjoying yourself. Do not overstress your body. If most of this ride turns out to be coasting, that's absolutely fine. Just get out there, enjoy yourself, and connect with the bike. You'll need your energy for tomorrow's workout.

Wednesday: Level I for 30 to 60 minutes at RPE 12. Eventually, this will become your key (hard) workout of the week. For now we're going to keep it easy and aerobic ("aerobic" means that your body has plenty of oxygen present while exercising; in other words, you're not out of breath). Pedal at a nice, steady pace. You shouldn't be out of breath, but you shouldn't feel like you're lollygagging out there.

Thursday: Rest.

Friday: Rest.

Saturday: Level I for 30 to 45 minutes at RPE 12. Conduct this workout the same way as you did on Tuesday; just add some extra time.

Sunday: *Level I for 45 to 60 minutes at RPE 13.* This is your long workout of the week. It requires a very gradual warmup process. Pedal easily for the first 5 minutes; then stop and do some easy stretching, focusing on muscles that are particularly sore or tight to you. Then move into the main portion of your workout. During your ride, maintain a heart rate between 130 and 160 beats per minute. You can and should walk your bike during portions of this ride (up hills, when you're out of breath, or when your heart rate exceeds 160). This achieves three things: You burn more fat (because you're not out of breath and reaching the point at which your body starts using sugar as fuel), the ride feels easier (so you can go longer), and you recover faster. After 4 weeks, you will build this ride up to 2 hours or more. Yes, that's right—2 hours!

Week 2

Monday: Rest.

Tuesday: Level I for 20 to 30 minutes at RPE 11. This is a "wake-up" ride. You had a nice rest day on Monday, and Wednesday you'll do a harder ride. You cannot rest for 2 days going into a hard ride, or you'll feel a little flat. (Here's an interesting fact: The riders in the Tour de France consistently remark that they feel better on the *second* stage of the tour, because they woke up their legs on the prologue, or first stage.) Conversely, neither should you ride too hard the day before a hard key workout—that'll just give you heavy legs! Just go out there, breathe in the fresh air, turn your legs over, and loosen up.

Wednesday: *Level II for 45 to 75 minutes at RPE 14 or 15.* This is your first hard workout of the program. After a thorough 30-minute warmup of easy to moderate pedaling and a couple of harder efforts of 10 to 15 seconds interspersed in there, begin riding for 10 minutes at a nice, steady, but comfortably challenging pace. If you feel strong—or if you started out this program in fairly good shape—you can really push the pace in these 10 minutes and ride at a 14 to 16 RPE. After the tempo portion, the 10 minutes when you push the pace, ride the remainder of this workout at a nice, comfortable speed, which corresponds to an RPE between 10 and 13.

Thursday: Rest. If you did yesterday's workout correctly, you'll need—and enjoy—this day off.

Friday: Rest. Yes, another off day. I want you to be energized for Saturday and Sunday.

Saturday: Level I for 45 minutes at RPE 11. This is a nice, steady aerobic ride. Make sure to warm up with easy pedaling for 10 to 15 minutes, and then transition into your ride by increasing the intensity to a comfortable but moderately challenging point.

Sunday: *Level I for 1 to 1¼ hours at RPE 12.* This is your long key workout of the week. The secret to this endurance ride is to maintain an even pace throughout so that you can go the distance and increase the duration each week without stressing your body too much.

Now that we've mapped out your plan, it's important to remember this maxim: Do your workouts *at your own pace.* You've likely heard that less is more, and indeed, that's a sound prescription. But it's equally important to establish momentum and see and feel results in the first few weeks, or you may be inclined to quit. So, while you should err on the

---

"Car Back; Rider Up"

A woman was exasperated with a cyclist because he was riding a little too far toward the middle of the road, and she was in a hurry. So, in a moment of blind fury—and at a blind right turn—she mashed down on the accelerator and attempted to pass the cyclist. But as she whirled around and into the oncoming lane, another car hit her head-on. Both drivers died, and so did the cyclist. It was a senseless end to three lives.

The number of cycling fatalities has risen steadily since 1996, and most experts believe that those numbers are increasing as the rift between bicyclists and drivers grows. Most of these tragedies and accidents might be avoided if there were more of an empathetic, "put yourself in their shoes" understanding between drivers and cyclists.

The biggest complaint that drivers have with you as a cyclist is that you might cavalierly ride in the middle of the road, which, intentionally or not, broadcasts to them, "I don't care about you! It's a glorious day to ride, and I'll take up as much of this road as I please!" That makes drivers angry and can lead to accidents later on. Granted, there are moments when you must ride near the middle of the road (to steer clear of road debris or to avoid parked-car doors that swing open), but it's imperative that you ride as close to the side of the road and as safely as possible.

---

side of caution when you're starting out, don't be afraid to push a little when you feel strong and confident. The flood of endorphins that rush through your body when you go fast will refuel your motivation like nothing else! Follow the program, but above all else, listen to your body and trust your instincts.

Stay Safe by Learning Basic Riding Skills

You are on a 10-week quest to reach a speed of 25 miles an hour. It's imperative that you remain as healthy, energetic, and strong as possible so that you can achieve that ambitious goal! One injury, crash, or illness can bring everything to a grinding halt. That will make fulfilling your quest far more difficult.

Next, like it or not, you must obey the same traffic laws that cars do—that's the law. This includes following the general flow of traffic and stopping at traffic lights and stop signs. Indeed, coming to a complete 3-second standstill at every stop sign is not entirely realistic. Most law-enforcement officials agree that it's sufficient to slow your bike to 2 to 3 miles an hour at stop signs while scanning both ways. Sprinting through stop signs on your bike, however, is stupid, careless, and undermines the broader car-cyclist rapport. Overtly breaking these laws is not only dangerous; it communicates to drivers that you feel exempt—above the law. This causes drivers to lose respect for all cyclists and can lead drivers to approach others more aggressively later on. Every action you take on your bike directly affects the well-being of other cyclists.

Finally, 9 out of 10 drivers are exceedingly patient, polite, and safe people that respect cyclists and extend them plenty of room and courtesy. Unfortunately and understandably, it's the errant, senseless, or dangerous driver that you remember. More often than not, when a driver does something that you feel is unsafe, they likely did it unknowingly. Give each driver the benefit of the doubt.

Ride Fast

When you ride a bike, you're cruising along with nothing between you and the pavement but the rubber on your tires, a pair of gloves, a helmet, and a thin layer of spandex. A bad crash can rattle more than your body; it can scare you away from the sport. Here are a few pointers to "keep the rubber side down."

First, always wear your helmet. According to the US Department of Transportation, roughly 700 people are killed each year and 51,000 are injured in cycling-related accidents. More than one-fourth of those killed are between 5 and 15 years; so parents, please snugly strap those helmets on your children.

Next, don't forget to use your rearview mirror. This simple device attaches to your sunglasses or helmet, and it allows you to safely monitor what's happening behind you without your having to turn your head, which can be a dangerous move on your bike.

Finally, pick your bike routes with care. Cycle on roads with the least vehicular traffic—this will keep you safer and make your cycling more fun, allowing you to focus on one thing: riding with passion in your drive for 25!

GATHERING MOMENTUM: WEEKS 3 AND 4

The world is wide, and I will not waste my life in friction when it could be turned into momentum.

—Frances Willard, American educator and reformer (1839–1898)

In weeks 1 and 2 of the training program, you established a little momentum—on your bike and in your mind. Now it's time to press those pedals, accelerate a bit, and feel the surge of excitement that comes from riding faster. At all costs, you must preserve and protect that precious momentum, because it is a titanic force, particularly when it comes to the bike.

mo·men·tum (mō-měn´-təm) *n. s.*

a. Impetus of a physical object in motion.

b. Impetus of a nonphysical process, such as an idea or a course of events: *Three weeks into the bike racing season, it appeared Hal was losing momentum because he wasn't taking enough rest days and his body was too exhausted!*

In physics, momentum refers to the amount of motion that an object has. Momentum is difficult to generate—it takes roughly nine times as much energy to get a body moving as to keep it moving. However, once an object has momentum, it becomes a mighty force. A cyclist moving at 25 miles an hour contains roughly the same amount of kinetic energy as 7 pounds of dynamite.

Visualize a period in which you experienced a string of stellar workouts. How did you feel? Energized? Compelled by a force outside yourself? You might have even developed a confident swagger. However, it's the intangible aspect of momentum, the "nonphysical process, such as an idea or a course of events," where the real power lies.

In athletics, momentum forges champions. Sports announcers will refer to a "shift in momentum," that point when one team begins to gather steam, the power surges into its players, their eyes get a little wild; the team becomes a juggernaut.

The power of momentum has altered the course of world events. In July 1943, the Russians repelled the Germans at the pivotal Battle of Kursk and turned the tide of World War II; Allied and Axis soldiers could feel the reverberations of Kursk thousands of miles away. The Allied victory suddenly felt inevitable—to both sides. In the 1960s, Martin Luther King catalyzed the civil rights movement and imbued it with such force of will that even after his death the momentum of civil rights stayed strong.

Momentum is a key ingredient of success in athletics. So, before you lose yours, let's dive into your new training program.

Your Training Plan for Weeks 3 to 10

The first 2 weeks of your training helped to prepare your body and mind for the increased demands of the next 8 weeks. Things will heat up now and get a little more challenging, but I believe that you're up to that challenge. And it's a true thrill when you begin to ride faster and with more power.

Weeks 3 through 10 follow the same template that was laid out in weeks 1 and 2; all that changes are the duration and intensity of your workouts. In other words, your long ride will take place every Sunday, but it will increase from 1 hour to 90 minutes, to 2 hours, and so on as the weeks progress.

You might think that doing the same thing week in and week out will get stale. Not on my watch! I promise we'll have plenty of variety in your program. But there's a real advantage to settling into a workout rhythm each week: You start to become habitual about riding your bike (and that's what you want). For example, you will begin to wake up naturally at 7 a.m. for that Tuesday tempo session once you've done so for several weeks.

Week 3

Monday: Rest. We'll keep Mondays as rest days. But as you increase the demands on your body with harder and longer workouts, these become "rest days plus," otherwise known as *active rest*. Passive rest is sitting on the couch and putting your feet up for the day; active rest is moving your body to speed the recovery process. This could take the form of a short, refreshing hike, a swim, or an easy bike ride—even a massage. These relaxing sessions actually speed recovery by flushing out your muscles, removing waste products while bringing in fresh oxygen and nutrients. The caveat is that you cannot stress your body on active recovery days. Keep your workouts very easy.

Tuesday: *Tempo ride for 1 hour at RPE 15 to 17.* In this session, warm up for at least 30 minutes; then stop and stretch for a few minutes. Get back on your bike, and from a rolling start, ride at a hard, sustained pace for 2 minutes at RPE 15 to 17. It's only 2 minutes, so hang in there! During this tempo portion, focus on staying strong mentally. Keep breathing deeply. Pedal smoothly. Don't allow the doubts and fears that can accompany pain to creep in. After the 2 minutes, ride easily for another 15 minutes, and then go into a 10-minute warm-down. Each week, add 1 minute to the tempo portion. For example, in week 4, do 3 minutes of tempo; in week 5, 4 minutes; and so on.

Wednesday: Strengthening and stretching for 40 minutes. Do the strength workout outlined in Chapter 1.

Thursday: Rest. It's essential to absorb the effects of your strenuous Tuesday session and Wednesday's strength training while resting up for your tough workouts on Saturday and Sunday.

Friday: Strengthening and stretching, 40 minutes. This is the same as Wednesday, but this session should feel at least 20 percent easier than that session. So cut either your number of repetitions or the amount of weight by 20 percent.

Saturday: *Intervals, 1 hour at RPE 14 to 16.* Perform this workout on flat or slightly downhill terrain. Start with a thorough 20-minute warmup that isn't too hard but is a little faster than your typical warmup. The more intense your workout, the more thorough your warmup needs to be—strenuous workouts push the limits of your muscles and your cardiovascular system. These systems must be fully primed to handle the demands of interval workouts, and that priming requires more time. Once you're warmed up, from a rolling start on your bike, spend 15 seconds building gradually into the interval. At the 15-second mark, you should be riding at 25 to 28 miles per hour. Try to hold that speed for a full 30 seconds. During the effort, focus on riding as powerfully as possible while staying as composed as you can. Rest for 3 minutes and repeat anywhere from two to four more times, depending on how you feel. Be sure to cool down completely after this workout by ramping down your intensity for 15 minutes.

Sunday: *Endurance, 1½ hours at RPE 12 to 14.* This ride should be completed at a comfortably challenging effort level; this is a Level I workout. Subjectively, you don't want to feel like you're slacking out there; you don't want to feel like you're pushing hard, either. This will put that staying power in your legs.

Week 4

Now we're going to bump up the duration of each session above while maintaining the intensities. This gentle ratcheting up will ensure steady progress without burning you out. (No burning out here, people!)

Monday: Rest.
Tuesday: 1¼-hour interval session at RPE 15 to 17.
Wednesday: 50-minute strength session.
Thursday: Rest.
Friday: 50-minute strength session.
Saturday: 1¼-hour interval session at RPE 14 to 16.
Sunday: 2-hour endurance session at RPE 12 to 14.

Week 5

Rest week. Now we're going to pull back and reduce all workouts by about 50 percent in duration. Also, you are going to do *no intense workouts*. This off week serves to consolidate all of your gains from the first 4 weeks and prepares your body and mind for the next 5.

Monday: Rest.
Tuesday: 40 minutes easy cycling at RPE 10 to 13.
Wednesday: 25-minute strength session.
Thursday: Rest.
Friday: 25-minute strength session.
Saturday: 40 minutes easy cycling at RPE 10 to 13.
Sunday: 1 hour easy cycling at RPE 10 to 13.

Week 6

Now we return to the next training cycle at a higher level than where you left off in week 4. (See why that rest week is so important now?) The details of each workout should follow week 3, but I encourage you to vary the terrain to keep things fresh. In other words, if you want to do Tuesday's interval session on a hilly course, go for it!

Monday: Rest.
Tuesday: 1½-hour interval session at RPE 15 to 17.
Wednesday: 1-hour strength session.
Thursday: Rest.
Friday: 1-hour strength session.
Saturday: 1½-hour interval session at RPE 14 to 16.
Sunday: 2¼-hour endurance session at RPE 12 to 14.

Week 7

Monday: Rest.
Tuesday: 1¾-hour interval session at RPE 15 to 17.
Wednesday: 1-hour strength session.

Thursday: Rest.
Friday: 1-hour strength session.
Saturday: 1¾-hour interval session at RPE 14 to 16.
Sunday: 2½-hour endurance session at RPE 12 to 14.

Week 8

This week, the durations are going to remain the same as those in week 7, but you are going to bump up the intensities to 10 percent above normal. For example, if you normally conduct your intervals at 150 beats per minute, increase that intensity to 165 beats per minute. The corresponding RPEs go up 1 or 2 per workout.

Monday: Rest.
Tuesday: 1¾-hour interval session at RPE 16 to 18.
Wednesday: 1-hour strength session.
Thursday: Rest.
Friday: 1-hour strength session.
Saturday: 1¾-hour interval session at RPE 15 to 17.
Sunday: 2½-hour endurance session at RPE 13 to 15.

Week 9

You're going to maintain the higher intensity levels of week 8, and you're going to add more duration. This is your toughest week. Give it everything you've got.

Monday: Rest.
Tuesday: 2-hour interval session at RPE 16 to 18.
Wednesday: 1-hour strength session.
Thursday: Rest.
Friday: 1-hour strength session.
Saturday: 2-hour interval session at RPE 15 to 17.
Sunday: 3-hour endurance session at RPE 13 to 15.

Week 10

A rest week to prepare for your time trial! It's well deserved! You've been busting your butt lately!

Monday: Rest.
Tuesday: 40 minutes easy cycling at RPE 10 to 13.
Wednesday: 25-minute strength session.
Thursday: Rest.
Friday: 25-minute strength session.
Saturday: 40 minutes easy cycling at RPE 10 to 13.
Sunday: 1 hour easy cycling at RPE 10 to 13.

Give Your Bike a Once-Over

Little will deflate your exercise motivation more than staring at an old, dusty bike, knowing that you haven't ridden in months. That little old two-wheeler can conjure up a litany of doubts and excuses. Most people give in to those negative emotions with a nice cool, comforting pint of Ben & Jerry's and a trip to the couch, thus extending the cycle of inactivity—and their waistline circumference—indefinitely.

But you can make your bike last years longer—and you can ride more easily— by performing some simple

(*Continued on page 62*)

Roll with the Seasons

Have you ever noticed that January 1 seems to be an awfully ill-timed date to embark on your New Year's health and fitness resolutions? You're essentially saying: "I'm going to become a better cyclist and lose these holiday love handles—in the dead of winter!" Few people emerge victorious after such proclamations.

Happily, there's a better way. By subtly modifying your weekly training plan as the seasons change, you can achieve markedly better cycling results, reduce exercise-induced injuries and pain, avoid frustrating ruts and plateaus, and boost your motivation.

It's a principle called *seasonal periodization,* and it is how most world-class cyclists design their annual training programs. It can help make achieving your cycling goal much more fun—and easier, too.

"The human body follows very precise 'circadian rhythms' throughout the year, which have been shown to follow the seasons," says Joe Friel, a nationally recognized fitness authority and the author of *The Cyclist's Training Bible.* "Periodization is an exercise concept in which your year is divided into periods, each having a specific approach based on weather conditions and how your body and mind are feeling, to produce the best possible results."

There is plenty of scientific evidence to support the efficacy of this approach; but it also makes good, logical sense, doesn't it? In winter, our desire to ride is at an annual low; in spring, we begin feeling more upbeat and motivated to work out; in summer, our bodies are most receptive to the effects of exercise; and in fall, we begin to mentally and physically wind down once again. The most effective cycling plan, therefore, follows these psychological and physiological rhythms and changes, or periodizes, throughout the year.

Winter

Setting your New Year's resolutions on January 1 is a social convention that makes little physiological, practical, or environmental sense. Have you ever noticed how much of a struggle it is to ride your bike through winter? Mother Nature is dead set against the proposition. Your motivational fire is low. Food-filled holidays seem to pop up every 2 to 3 weeks, and your metabolism is at a standstill. (How do you know? Your body is ruthlessly transforming every molecule of holiday food into love handles.) It's unnatural, impractical, and unnecessary for you to be out there slogging through cycling workouts during the cold and wet winter months.

Try this approach instead: During winter, keep your riding intensity and frequency down. No more than 3 days a week and no harder than 50 to 70 percent of your maximum heart rate. (To calculate your maximum heart rate in beats per minute, subtract your age from 220.)

In other words, just get out there, keep it easy, and relax. Riding like this in winter will keep you healthy and energized while establishing a nice aerobic base of fitness upon which you can—and should—build.

Spring

As the weather warms and the days grow longer, most people experience a noticeable increase in their desire and willingness to ride. Mother Nature is now your exercise ally. Spring is the time to gently ramp up your cycling program.

Keep the composition of your plan the same, but pick one workout a week where you really challenge yourself. For example, the duration of your Tuesday ride might remain at 30 minutes but now include two to three tempo portions in which you ride a little faster for 2 minutes at a time. Because you took it easy on your body in winter, it will be more receptive to the strenuous, fitness-building workouts in spring.

Summer

This is when you should really get busy on your body and make the serious drive for 25. Invest the most time and energy in your riding in summer. Now is the time of the year to push yourself, so put even more oomph into those key workouts. Add more climbing to your program. Just be sure to give more focus to rest days, because your body will be working very hard. These two adjustments will pay enormous dividends in your health, weight loss, and speed!

(Continued)

(*Cont.*)

Fall

As the days progressively cool off and shorten, it's time to ease off the accelerator, as well. If you've followed the seasonal program, then you will have a wonderful base of cardiovascular fitness upon which to sail into fall. You don't want to stop riding completely; just rein it in. The fall and winter months allow you to refresh your body and mind so that you can elevate your game the following spring. Your training plan in fall

maintenance on it every few months. You will enjoy riding more on a well-maintained bike, because it will carry you faster, farther, and smoother; its parts work more efficiently than a neglected bike's. (In other words, you gain a significant advantage over your buddies on that weekend ride if your bike is functioning better!) A poorly lubricated chain alone can sap 1 mile an hour from you. You can't afford to give away a mile an hour on a dirty chain in your drive for 25!

A well-maintained bike is also safer. A bicycle that hasn't been cared for can give out at precisely the wrong time. For example, if your headset or steering tube is not adjusted properly, you could lose complete steering control of your bike.

You have two choices when undertaking bicycle maintenance: You can drop it off at your local bike shop and have them do all the work (which can be costly), or you can do it yourself (which can take more time). The best route to go may be a combination of the two: Twice a year, bring your bike into the shop, and then periodically make sure that all's well with your ride yourself. That way, trained bike mechanics can do the general checkups and major work, and you can keep up the basic maintenance.

The first step is to give your bike a quick once-over to make sure everything is in good working order. Begin by walking around the bike and examining the frame for dents and cracks. Stand over the front wheel, nestle the wheel between your knees, then grab hold of the handlebars and wiggle them back and forth. The handlebars should feel solid and shouldn't give relative to the wheel. This maneuver checks the should be somewhere between your winter and spring programs in terms of intensity and duration.

Follow this seasonal program and you'll be training just like the pros: You'll enjoy your riding more, you'll achieve better long-term results, and each year you will celebrate a firmer belly and fewer aches—rather than bellyache about another year gone by!

headset, which is what steers your bike. You don't want your headset coming loose during a ride, as you will lose all control immediately.

Next, check the integrity of your tires—are there any cuts, or is there debris lodged in them? Flats deflate more than your tires; they deflate your spirit. Have your tires been on that bike since the disco era? Do they need to be replaced? Your tires are where the rubber meets the road, so spend the $20 per tire if you need new ones—go for high-pressure tires with antipuncture Kevlar belts.

Make sure your tires are pumped up to the proper pressure (which is indicated on the side of the tire itself). Well-inflated tires help you ride faster by reducing rolling resistance and also decrease the risk of flats, because harder tires deflect debris better. Generally, road bikes require

90 to 120 pounds per square inch (psi).

Check your brakes. Spin each wheel, and then grab the brake levers and pull hard. Do they stop the wheel completely? Spin your wheel again, and this time make sure that it's straight, or true.

Look over your drivetrain, which is comprised of the chain, chain rings, freewheel, and all those little moving parts near the derailleur (the gear shifter). Does everything look to be in good working order? In other words, is anything skip-

ping, clicking, clanking, or creaking? (You don't want your bike doing any of those things, as they usually signal a problem!) Are there layers of dirt and grime on there dating back to the Pleistocene era? If so, clean your drivetrain, using a basic engine degreaser, which can be purchased at most hardware stores for about $3, to reduce friction and therefore allow the bike to roll more easily. Once your drivetrain is clean, it's time to oil your chain. Use a more viscous, bike-specific lube such as TriFlow rather than WD-40, which can dry out your chain over time.

Next, check all the bolts on your bike and tighten them. Two areas to particularly focus on are the handlebar binder bolt, which holds the handlebars in place, and the seat binder bolt, which does the same for your seat. Exerting the right torque is important, particularly on more delicate frame materials such as carbon, which can crack if you overtighten bolts. To learn the proper pressure, have an experienced mechanic show you.

Finally, it's time to shine your bike to a high gloss! A clean bike looks better—and believe me, you'll be more inspired to ride fast if it looks good. Use your garden hose to spray off your frame; then dry it with an old towel. Apply a basic car wax to your bike's main tubes to protect them against rain and make you look more like a pro as you sail by others. Voilà! A machine fit to carry you at supersonic speeds!

8 mph: Get Fit

Most people are not properly positioned on their bicycles; that makes riding more painful and uncomfortable and saps much of your power. Subtle changes in how you are fitted on your bicycle can pay tremendous dividends in your drive for 25.

Your aim is to achieve what is known as biomechanical synchronicity: the point at which all muscle groups of your lower body—your quadriceps, hamstrings, calves, and gluteus maximus—are working together in harmony to move your bike forward fluidly. Achieving biomechanical synchronicity is a sublime feeling.

Andy Pruitt, EdD, director of the Boulder Center for Sports Medicine in Colorado, is one of the nation's leading authorities on bicycle positioning. He sums up proper bike fit as "a marriage between the human body, which is somewhat adaptable, and a machine that is somewhat adjustable."

You needn't go through complex machinations to achieve the ideal fit; biomechanical synchronicity can be had in three simple steps.

Step One: Frame Size

"The first step to proper bike positioning is to make sure you have the right bike frame size," says Paul Swift, eight-time US national cycling champion and master bike-fitting technician. "Stand over your bicycle's top tube (between the seat and the handlebar). The general rule of thumb for road bikes is roughly 1 inch of clearance between your crotch and the frame. For a mountain bike, you should have 2 to 6 inches."

Step Two: Saddle Height

"Correct saddle height—the distance from the pedal axle to the top of the seat—is one of the most important factors in bike positioning," says

How to Fix a Flat

If you get a flat tire, your first order of business is to get off the road and park yourself in a safe, comfortable location. Don't panic or feel anxious; everyone gets flat tires. Take a deep breath and a drink of water.

To begin, remove the wheel. Using tire irons, loosen one side of your tire and remove the tube. Inspect the tire to see what caused the flat. Use your fingers to carefully feel the inside of the tire casing for any sharp object that may have punctured the tube. If you miss any such object, it will quickly puncture the new tube, so take your time here!

Once you're sure the tire is clear, partially inflate your fresh tube, and carefully insert it into the tire. Then roll the tire back onto the rim, making absolutely sure not to pinch the tube inside. Make sure the tire bead (which lines the outside of your tire and hooks it into the rim) is securely fastened into the rim all the way around the wheel on both sides. Pump the tire up a little to make sure it's securely fastened into the rim. Then inflate the tire to its recommended pressure—and you're on your way.

It's important to note that your newly installed tire is a little more susceptible to flats (you may not have reinstalled it perfectly), so pay extra attention to it until you arrive home. Then have an expert mechanic reinstall the tire. (It's well worth the expense.)

Investing in high-quality name-brand tubes and tires—such as Panaracer, Vittoria, or Specialized—will dramatically reduce the frequency of flats. You can also investigate air-free tires that allege flat-free performance for life. Visit www.airfreetires.com for more information. It's important to carry new tubes with you in your spare kit when you ride. The last thing you want to happen is to get a flat and reach for your spare tube, only to realize that that one is flat, as well!

John Howard, seven-time national champion, three-time Olympian, and founder of the Cycling School of Champions in San Diego. According to Howard, your saddle height should be set so your legs almost fully extend at the bottom of each pedal stroke. To check for correct leg extension, while sitting on your seat, rotate your pedals to the 12 o'clock and 6 o'clock positions. The bottom leg (6 o'clock position) should have a slight bend in the knee, roughly 30 degrees. "Your hips should not rock back and forth when you pedal—that means your legs have to stretch too far to reach the bottom of the pedal stroke. If your hips rock, lower your saddle," Howard says.

Step Three: Shoe/Cleat Alignment

The position of your cleats on your cycling shoes determines the comfort of your feet, ankles, knees, hips, and back. Why? Because once you clip into your pedals, the path that your leg tracks during the pedal stroke is locked in. Misaligned cleats send stress from your foot to your lower back with every pedal stroke. A proper cleat alignment will also help transfer the maximum power from your legs to the pedals.

"When mounting cleats, you want your feet to feel straight when clipped into the pedals," says Sean Drake, an exercise physiologist who works with the US national triathlon and cycling teams. "When setting . . . cleat position, the ball of your foot should be directly over the pedal axle. Side-to-side adjustment is based on personal preference—usually the narrower stance, the better, but start somewhere in the middle and see what feels right."

For optimal cleat positioning, visit a bicycle shop that utilizes the RAD, or Rotational Adjustment Device. If you purchase your bike from the bike shop, ask that they include this service for free. If you already own your bike, this will likely run you about $25. It's well worth the expense. This tool is widely regarded as one of the most reliable methods for setting the cleat position on the cycling shoe and allowing for the rider's natural gait. It may take some time to find the ideal cleat position. The rule of thumb is to continue adjusting your cleats until you feel no torsional, or twisting, stress in your legs as you pedal. The cardinal rule when getting your bike fitted is to listen to your body.

9 mph: Develop a Deeper Drive to Ride

For many of us, exercise is boring, just another task on our daily to-do list. One word we use for physical activity is *workout.* We view exercise as another form of work! No wonder so many of us do almost anything we can to avoid it. We work all day; who wants to come home and put in more?

When you hear the word *exercise,* what comes to mind? Your first reaction speaks volumes about your relationship with physical activity and therefore influences your motivation to ride. "Boring," "painful," and "time-consuming" flash across most of our mental screens, and the only way you will boost your long-term exercise motivation is to change the way you view cycling and to associate pleasure with it more than pain. That begins with making a shift in your attitude and your approach. The French novelist Marcel Proust once said: "The real voyage of discovery consists not in seeking new landscapes, but in seeing with new eyes."

This is how you should approach your cycling from now on. These 10 weeks aren't just about building up to 25 miles per hour, not just about hitting a target; they are about rolling along in an idyllic reverie and seeing the world with new eyes, about learning to ride for the sheer pleasure of it.

Our vision of physical activity has ebbed and flowed over the past 50 years. In the 1950s, scientists were beginning to prove the wide-ranging health benefits of working out, but people viewed it more as an enigmatic activity than anything else: When someone was seen running down the street, onlookers stretched to find out who might be chasing them. Not until Jim Fixx, the running pioneer, ushered in the jogging and aerobics revolution of the 1970s did exercise take on a deeper personal meaning to people. It became fashionable to work out—and although people donned unfashionable tube socks and headbands, millions of them took up exercise.

In the 1980s and 1990s, physical activity mirrored the times: Exercise was about looking good. Having a fit, svelte body was a status symbol that broadcast an image of power and control. People were externally motivated to stay fit, and they worked out because of what it did for them rather than how it made them feel.

Today, exercise has been sadly demoted to its lowest level yet: burning calories. Add that perception of physical activity to people's busier work schedules, and we can better understand why the average American exercises fewer than 90 minutes per week and why America is the fattest nation in the world. The US surgeon general, David Satcher, MD, PhD, has designated obesity as an epidemic and, in doing so, has quantified its annual costs to America: 300,000 deaths and over $50 billion in elevated health insurance premiums.

Riding your bike should be about letting go, pedaling out into the world, getting sunshine on your face, and having fun. It should be easy, in the moment, and playful. If you follow that maxim and you trust and listen to your body, you'll shift your vision of exercise and unleash the same motivations that sustain the belly fires of champion cyclists.

"Human beings have 'hardwired' psychological reasons behind choices we make," says Timothy Noakes, MD, author of *Lore of Running*. "Research shows that people who work out regularly have predominantly positive associations with physical activity. Most of us fundamentally do not enjoy exercise, which almost instinctually compels us to avoid it. But if you can learn to redefine how you see and perform workouts, you can improve your 'hardwired' perceptions of fitness, and that leads to better lifetime results," he says.

According to many experts, the solution may be to develop your intrinsic motivation.

"Intrinsic motivation—or performing a task for its own sake—is the most powerful way to change behavior," says Jay Kimiecik, PhD, a professor at Miami University in Oxford, Ohio, and the author of *The Intrinsic Exerciser*. This is particularly true of riding your bike.

"Doing a behavior for its own sake or learning how to enjoy a (healthy) behavior is not generally part of health promotion," he says. "It's usually, 'If you want to live a long life and reduce your risk of disease, you better figure out how to do these behaviors or you're going to die at an early age. . . .' The main difference with this approach is getting people to zoom in on their feelings and thoughts before, during, and after an exercise experience."

This is precisely what kids do. They ride because it makes them feel good.

This inside-out approach to physical activity is what cultivates an intrinsic motivation; unfortunately, this is precisely the opposite of how many of us approach exercise. We tend to be destination oriented when it comes to our bodies: We ride our bikes to burn calories. We have to turn that around.

If you take the outside-in approach, external factors—such as poor weather—will more easily derail your cycling efforts. When you build an intrinsic motivation, you will seek to ride more often and with more passion.

"Unless you become an intrinsic exerciser, things in life will keep coming up and will make it easier and easier for you not to exercise," says Dr. Kimiecik. "As an intrinsic exerciser, you'll figure out ways to overcome these various barriers."

The first step to developing an intrinsic exercise motivation is to shift your focus from the outcome to the process. While it's important to keep your eye on the prize—in this case, hitting 25 miles per hour—you must stay focused on short-term goals that relate to participation (for example, how many times you train in a week, what types of rides you'll do, and so on). That way, weight loss and speed come as a result of the participation-centric focus. In other words, you'll be thinking intrinsically.

Keep your focus on doing your best each day—not on where you'll be in the future. This begins with setting a clear goal for each workout—too vague a goal may result in your focus shifting to the boredom or discomfort of the session. If your goal for a ride is to improve your pedaling efficiency, then focus on your breathing, using graceful technique, relaxing your muscles, and moving your legs through the full 360 degrees of the pedal stroke. Key in on pedaling like a pro and the thrill that comes along with rolling stronger, smoother, and faster.

The next step to developing an intrinsic motivation is to hone your ability to concentrate during rides. Mental focus can help you experience "flow," which trainer and author Mihaly Csikszentmihalyi (*Flow: The Psychology of Optimal Experience*, p. 108) defines as "an optimal psychological state characterized by an intense absorption in a workout, a clear sense of your goals, and a feeling of letting go." To increase your flow during cycling, concentrate on a deep, smooth, and rhythmic breathing pattern, such as exhaling every other time your right foot sweeps down.

Pedal Power

In any given 30-minute ride, you will turn your pedals roughly 2,000 times. Honing your pedal stroke efficiency by a mere 5 percent may not sound significant, but extrapolated over a half-hour ride, it can net huge dividends.

To improve your pedaling action, shift your focus. Since your foot naturally performs the push-down portion of the motion—with the help of gravity—key in on smoothing the other parts of the circle.

"Most people pedal with pressure only on the down stroke, a habit picked up over years of riding as kids," says John Howard, seven-time national champion, three-time Olympian, and founder of the Cycling School of Champions in San Diego. "The best way I've found to optimize my pedal stroke is to 'kick across' the top of the pedal circle and 'drag my foot' along the bottom." In other words, when your foot approaches the top of the pedal stroke, push your foot over the top. As your foot approaches the bottom of the pedal stroke, visualize wiping something from the bottom of your shoe and "drag" your foot through the bottom part of the stroke.

Another key element of efficient pedaling is to relax your legs: Let them sweep over the pedal stroke rather than trying to force it. If your muscles are tight or flexed, that will inhibit the smoothness of your pedal motion. There is one technique drill that works wonders on smoothing things out: pedaling with one leg at a time. That will encourage you to move the pedal in full circles and sensitize you to dead spots in your stroke almost immediately. On flat terrain, simply pedal with one leg, keeping the circle as smooth as possible. If you can learn to pedal smoothly for a minute or more with one leg, you've taken another step toward 25!

After your workout, take a moment to note how your body felt and what went through your mind. What felt good? What physical and mental strategies helped you stay centered on each moment? What can you do to improve the ride the next time out? Analyzing your cycling session shortly after the fact and framing things in a positive way will change your vision of riding by improving your awareness of the exercise experience.

Finally, if you want to enjoy cycling as much as possible, it's essential to balance the challenge of the session with your current skill level. In other words, design a workout goal that is neither so challenging that it makes you suffer nor so easy that it makes you apathetic. Challenging yourself subtly each time you work out is a thrilling feeling and helps you shift your vision of exercise by developing inside-out motivation.

10 mph: Listen to Your Heart

It takes the guesswork out of cycling by effectively serving as a personal trainer on your wrist. It reduces perceived exertion during cycling by keeping you in more appropriate intensity zones. It teaches you how to pace yourself. It can boost your athletic performance by reducing long-term fatigue associated with repeated overexertion. It can minimize the onset of exercise-induced illness and injury. And it can leave you feeling fresher after exercise so that you can be more productive in your daily life.
But no, it doesn't slice, dice, and julienne.

"It" is a heart rate monitor, and learning how to use one will put at least 1 more mile an hour into those legs!

These testaments are telling.

• Six-time Ironman champion and fitness author Dave Scott: "Every question I ever had about exercise or training was answered when I bought, and began using, a heart rate monitor."

• Edmund R. Burke, PhD, the late nationally renowned exercise physiologist: "The heart rate monitor has the potential to revolutionize training for health, fitness, and competition."

• Bruce Chapman, dad and regular guy: "With the benefit of my heart rate monitor as a source of feedback, I'm beginning to notice material improvements in my cycling. I am riding faster at a lower average heart rate, and my heart rate is dropping much farther and faster during my cooldown. That encouragement makes my whole routine more fun. I am also using more body fat as fuel; I've lost 10 pounds in 3 weeks—without killing myself to do it!"

Here's how and why it works.

A heart rate monitor is a simple device: A wireless strap goes around your chest and transmits your heart rate to a watch that displays a constant, accurate display. Why is heart rate so important? Because it's a precise gauge of how hard your body is working when you ride your bike—or do any physical activity, for that matter. How hard you work out day to day, week to week, is everything in achieving optimal fitness. If you have a goal (improved health and fitness, fat loss, or riding 25 miles an hour), you will get there faster, easier, and more efficiently if you exercise in the right zones.

Top endurance athletes only periodically exceed their aerobic maximum—the point at which you run out of air and your body shifts from using fat as its primary fuel source to sugar—during workouts. (To determine your aerobic maximum in heartbeats per minute, you must use a heart rate monitor. Here's an easy way to do that: After a thorough warmup, increase the pace of your ride until you begin to run out of breath. Now ride at that pace and no harder for another 1 minute, and record your heart rate.) That's how they continually improve—they get fit without fatigue, which means they feel good during workouts, they absorb the benefits of their exercise, and they can work out more consistently, over time, with fewer injuries and less fatigue. This leads to faster progress, soaring confidence, greater energy, and a desire to ride more often. This is known as the "aerobic cycle." When people go anaerobic during exercise, they break down their bodies, they get tired or injured, and they plateau more easily. Then what happens? They lose motivation and throw in the towel after a few weeks. A heart rate monitor will help you harness the aerobic cycle and have more fun on your bike rides.

Heart rate monitoring is a technology that transcends age, ability, and fitness level. Finnish Olympic cross-country skiers, Kenyan runners, casual walkers, even my dad! Whoever you are, whatever your fitness disposition or goal, paying heed to your heart rate monitor will give you more benefit from your exercise time.

Calculating Your Target Heart Rate Zones

One of the biggest myths in the fitness world is that you have to work hard and be out of breath to boost your fitness. Although it may seem counterintuitive, it is almost always better to stay below the point where you lose control of your breath; that is, below your maximum heart rate. When you ride this way, you burn more fat and cycling feels easier, so you're inclined to do it more often. Over time, you become more aerobically fit, meaning your body becomes more efficient at working out, because it's more efficient at using oxygen.

By training in more aerobic zones, you can get fit without fatigue. That leads to faster progress, increased confidence, greater energy, and greater devotion to the exercise regimen—the aerobic cycle. When you work out at easier effort levels—below your maximum heart rate—you feel good during your workouts and finish them feeling invigorated. On the other hand, if you work out at your maximum heart rate, your body cannot breathe fast enough for you to continue at that pace. You're out of breath; your lungs burn. You finish your workout feeling ready for a Snickers bar and a 2-hour nap.

So rather than exercising at your maximum heart rate, you should train at your ideal training zones (also called target heart rate zones). In order to train in the zone, so to speak, you need to know your maximum heart rate. A number of factors influence your maximum heart rate, including your age, genetics, fitness level, and overall health. You can find your true maximum heart rate by exercising to exhaustion and recording what your heart rate is at that point. This can be dangerous, however, and should be done only under the watchful eye of a physician. For our purposes, you can determine your approximate maximum heart rate by subtracting your age from 220. Write that number here:

Maximum heart rate (MHR): _____

You will use this number as the basis for your workouts. Think of your maximum heart rate as a speed limit of sorts. Sure, you can exercise at your speed limit, but doing so makes your engine consume more fuel, which means you'll run out more quickly.

Tempo

These workouts last anywhere from 2 to 8 minutes and require five nice, gradual 15-minute warmups, which cause your heart rate to exceed no more than 50 percent of your aerobic maximum. When you exercise in this zone, your subjective feeling is comfortably challenging. In other words, you're working, but you're not out of control. Your heart rate should be at 60 to 70 percent of your maximum heart rate during the tempo portion and should hover around 50 percent of your MHR for the remainder of the ride.

Intervals

Intervals can last anywhere from 30 seconds to 2 minutes and should be performed only after at least 4 weeks of consistent, injury-free cycling. They help you focus on increasing your speed. When you're doing an interval session, your heart rate should be at 70 to 80 percent of the maximum and come to a complete recovery during the rest portion.

Endurance

These workouts should be conducted at a steady pace. Your heart rate should hover in the range of 50 to 60 percent of the maximum and should not exceed 130 beats per minute. These rides build aerobic fitness and the staying power you need to hit your mark of 25 miles per hour.

Remember this timeless fitness maxim: Harder is not better; smarter is better. Train in your zones. For more information and to review research about heart rate monitors, visit www.polarusa.com.

Chapter Summary: Your Assignments

• Write your training program over the next 8 weeks into your daily planner, and assign a high priority to every key workout.

• Purchase a few sets of dumbbells for home use, and begin a strength-training program for as little as 30 minutes twice a week.

• Spend some time learning the various parts of your bike—and tuning it up. (You can also bring it to the local bike shop!)

• Find an expert to fit you perfectly on your bike. This is nonnegotiable. You must achieve the right position on your bicycle if you want to avoid pain and injury and ride up to your potential.

• Practice pedaling as smoothly as possible through the complete circle, or 360 degrees.

• Get a heart rate monitor, calculate your maximum heart rate (MHR), and design your workouts as percentages of that all-important number.

GAINING SPEED: WEEKS 5 AND 6

Success usually comes to those who are too busy to be looking for it.
—Henry David Thoreau (1817–1862)

If you're like me, you don't like to waste time when you work out. When I train, my objective is to get the greatest benefit and have as much fun as I can. After all, if you're going to take the time out of your day and get out there and sweat, you want to feel that you're exercising in the right way and getting the most out of it, right?

11 mph: Experience the Perfect Ride Every Time

Many people tend to exercise with their heads, and sometimes that can get in the way of fully enjoying themselves and getting the most from workouts. Relative to exercise, our minds begin to kick in with the pre-workout mental debate, which goes something like this: "Should I ride?" "I'm too tired." "What's on TV?" As we begin our workout, our minds tend to shift into overdrive as we focus on issues at work or the boredom and strenuousness of the workout. To fully enjoy your cycling, you must learn to quiet your mind. That's not to say you shouldn't sort through important life issues when you're pedaling away; you should. The point is that you should experience extended periods on your bike in which you have no thoughts and during which you're just sailing along under the power of your legs. If you can capture that childlike passion for the bike, you'll ride faster, longer, and for the rest of your life.

How you ride influences how you view the sport—and all physical activity, for that matter. If you want to shift that vision to the positive, you must ride differently. Here is an example of how to perform 30-minute workouts over the next 2 weeks that will begin to hardwire a more motivating view of cycling—and help you get the best results from your ride.

First, if you arrive home from work mentally and physically exhausted, it's imperative to undergo a brief transition to the bike. Research shows that after a long day of thinking and analyzing, our brain waves are predominantly beta waves, which indicate higher-level mental functioning. While that frame of mind helps us problem-solve at work, it is not conducive to physical activity. You need to be a little more mindless when you ride your bike, or your analytical brain function will get in the way. The best thing you can do to transition from work to play is to take a 10-minute hot shower. This may sound strange, but it works. Mentally, the water washes away fatigue; physiologically, it invigorates your body by increasing metabolism and bloodflow to your muscles.

After your preworkout shower, play some of your favorite music on your headset or stereo. Listening to relaxing, motivating music is one of the simplest and most immediate ways to shift your vision to exercise and to expand those brain waves from short, choppy beta to long, sweeping alpha.

Next, seek out a beautiful, inspiring workout venue; if you must drive to a striking spot that has less vehicular traffic, do it. Remember that what you associate with cycling will determine how fast you ride and whether exercise becomes a permanent part of your life; where you choose to ride exerts great influence, as well.

Begin your perfect ride by clearing your mind of expectations, limits, and rules: There are none in this particular ride. This workout can last 5 minutes or a full hour. Leave the watch and the heart rate monitor

behind, and let your heart call the shots. As you know, I strongly encourage you to monitor your heart rate during workouts in order to get the greatest benefit from your training. However, there are times— say, once every couple of weeks—when you should liberate yourself from exercise technology, rules, and guidelines and just go out there and soak up the scenery and be fully present in each moment.

Pedaling leisurely for the first few minutes and breathing deeply into your belly will oxygenate your muscles and your brain. With each inhalation, picture the air entering your lungs and swirling through your bloodstream to fuel your muscles, and feel your energy rise and your senses come alive. With each exhalation, visualize your muscle tension melting away. Gradually increase your effort—but do so slowly. Stay focused on your breathing, keep your mind clear, maintain a comfortable pace, and remain as present in the moment as you can. If you begin to feel negative or distracting thoughts creep in, slowly and deliberately brush them offscreen, and as you ride, spend a few moments taking stock of all the positive things in your life: your health, your children, or how fortunate you are to be alive right now.

Start to deepen the connection you feel with your bike. It's not merely a mass of metal beneath you; it's an extension of your body. Smooth out your pedal stroke, consciously relax every muscle in your body, and get your balance directly over the frame. Let your body decide whether you push yourself. Be honest with what you can do that day. If you feel good, push it a little bit.

(*Continued on page 84*)

81

Power-Breathe

Ever notice how a few nice, deep breaths instantly improve your mental and physical state? Try it right now, and you'll see what I mean. Deep breathing causes positive physiological changes in your body, and learning to breathe more efficiently is one of the most surefire ways to improve your cycling performance.

In a study published in *The Lancet,* a British medical journal, researchers at the University of Pavia in Italy showed that people who underwent focused deep-breathing exercises before and during exercise showed higher levels of blood oxygen and were able to perform far better on exercise tests.

The more oxygen you have pumping through your bloodstream during rides, the better you'll perform and the easier the exercise will feel, because your muscles need oxygen in order to work during exercise, and your bloodflow supplies it. Increase the oxygen in your blood, and your muscles work more efficiently. Unfortunately, most of us don't realize anywhere near the power of breathing, on our bikes or elsewhere.

Purge the Fat, Lower the Blood Pressure

The Italian researchers also reported that "low blood oxygen may impair skeletal muscle and metabolic function, and lead to higher levels of perceived exertion, muscle atrophy, and exercise intolerance." Lance Armstrong, who recently won his seventh consecutive Tour de France competition, processes roughly 6 liters of oxygen per minute (80 ml/kg) during exercise. Compare that to 3½ to 4 liters of oxygen per minute (35 to 40 ml/kg) for the average person.

Power breathing will boost the amount of oxygen you can process. This will enhance your fat-burning metabolism, because you're providing your body with extra oxygen (your body needs plenty of oxygen to burn fat). As a result, you'll get rid of that extra flab quicker—everyone loves that! Power breathing also makes cycling feel easier, because your body isn't constantly struggling for air, which gives you a greater sense of control and confidence during rides. Still, the main benefit of power breathing during exercise is that it lowers blood pressure and stress levels.

When you exercise too strenuously, your body releases adrenaline as a result of high physical stress, or what is known as the "sympathetic response." You know the feeling: As you increase your workout intensity, you begin to lose your breath, you start panting, and you can feel the pain markedly increase in your body. This causes your blood pressure to rise and, over time, can result in physical fatigue, sometimes known as "adrenal exhaustion." I've been there, and take it from me—it's not fun.

Breathing deeply—in through your nose and out through your mouth—engages a relaxation or parasympathetic response, which decreases your blood pressure, lowers perceived stress levels, improves circulation, lowers your pulse rate, diminishes oxygen consumption, and can create a sense of mental and spiritual well-being.

Elite Athletes and the Relaxation Response

Just watch the best athletes before their major athletic events. They are completely immersed in breathing rituals. Deep breathing can almost instantly center you by oxygenating your brain and your body, preparing you for peak physical and mental performance. In addition, top athletes will focus on breathing during competitions: If you watch Lance Armstrong's time trials, you will notice how his belly literally pumps up and down and how his breathing pattern stays steady and strong. Lance knows that his performance relies on oxygen getting to his muscles! Breathing like this can help you break through to phenomenal levels of performance on your bike. Here's how to do it.

1. Sit erect, and place your hands lightly over your stomach. Close your eyes and clear your mind.

2. Breathe in through your nose. As your lungs fill up with air, you want to expand your abdomen outward. It should feel like you're breathing right into your belly. Your hands should be moving outward. The full inhalation should take at least 10 seconds—yes, that long! Your abdominals should expand as much as or more than your chest. Visualize the oxygen swirling into your bloodstream.

(Continued)

(Cont.)

3. When you've fully inhaled, breathe in a little more, and even a little more. Go on, challenge yourself. This will expand your lung capacity dramatically. Now, hold that full inhalation for 3 seconds.

4. As you slowly exhale out of your mouth, visualize every bit of your mental and physical stress dissolving with that breath. The exhalation should take 5 seconds or more.

You ought to feel pretty good now! During rides, you won't be breathing that slowly, but the idea is the same—keep your breathing deep, relaxed, and rhythmic. Remember that the point at which you lose your breath

When you feel that you've had enough, slow to an easier pace, shake out your muscles, do some easy stretching, and take a few cleansing breaths. Dismount your bike, reach to the sky while inhaling, and slowly lower your arms while exhaling. You may want to lie on the grass, look up at the sky, and relish how good you feel. Why all these machinations? Because you need to fall in love with the bike again. You need to shift your vision of exercise. For the next 2 weeks, approach your workouts in this playful, present, and introspective fashion, and you'll discover new joys of working out and break through to new levels of performance. Do this and your motivation will also soar.

12 mph: Stay Fueled—Don't Bonk!

You're starting to ride faster now, and that means you're burning up a lot more fuel. For a 160-pound man, riding at a mere 12 miles an hour burns almost 500 calories an hour. The upshot of this is that you may notice some nice changes in your body: less fat, more muscle. The downside is that you may become more tired in your daily life—and during workouts you will become more susceptible to the dreaded "bonk."

It's a four-letter word in athletic circles—something to be avoided at all costs. When it hits you during rides, you get light-headed, you lose during exercise is generally when you shift from using body fat to using muscle sugar as fuel. That chemical process is not efficient and can ultimately lead to muscle breakdown, fatigue, and depressed immunity.

The next time you ride your bike, focus on breathing in through your nose and into your belly, not into your chest. As you gradually increase your effort, use your breathing to calm yourself, to gain progressively more control over your body and mind. This is what the best athletes do during world-record performances and what you must do on your bike.

your focus (and if you're like me, you get cranky), and your legs slowly and inexorably grind to a halt.

Bonking, as a physical phenomenon, became better known in the late 1980s when marathon runners reported hitting the wall at mile 20 or thereabouts in the 26.2-mile event. Research later verified that those people were simply running out of glycogen, the body's primary energy source during physical activity.

You'll see it in bike races such as the Tour de France. All of a sudden, a top professional will crack. He'll run out of gas completely, and all he can do to finish the stage is turn the pedals slowly until he reaches the line. When you bonk, that's it. There's no coming back until the next day.

While most of us don't run the risk of hitting the wall in our daily workouts, we've all had less-than-stellar sessions and wondered why. But by making slight alterations to how and what you eat before, during, and after bike rides, you will spare yourself from bonking and enjoy your workouts more.

First and foremost, you need extra carbohydrates to provide the fuel for exercise and recovery, vitamins and minerals to help convert those carbohydrates to usable energy, and protein for adding new muscle. Plus, you need some fat to keep cell membranes healthy and to produce important hormones. The best way to meet these nutritional needs is not with a gym bag full of energy bars and Gatorade. It's with a balanced diet fine-tuned for your exercise goals and calorie needs.

Let's talk first about energy production. Your body's main fuel currency is a substance called adenosine triphosphate, or ATP for short. All fuel—carbohydrates, fats, and proteins—need to be converted to ATP before it can be burned for energy.

During rest, the body gets slightly more than half of its ATP from fatty acids, and the rest comes from carbohydrates, along with a small percentage of amino acids from protein breakdown. During physical activity, the body adjusts its mixture of fuels. Your muscles never use just one single fuel, and how much of a specific fuel they use during exercise depends on the duration and intensity of the activity and the degree of conditioning.

During exertion, glucose that is stored in the liver and muscles as glycogen is released into the bloodstream. Your muscles use both of these glycogen stores to fuel their work. When glycogen is depleted, the muscles become fatigued. Glycogen depletion usually occurs about 2 hours after the onset of intense activity.

Studies have confirmed that high-carbohydrate diets enhance endurance by enlarging glycogen stores. In one study, runners eating a diet high in fat and protein and low in carbohydrates had a maximum endurance time of 57 minutes, those getting about 50 percent of their calories from carbohydrates lasted 114 minutes, and those eating a high-carbohydrate diet (comprising 83 percent of calories) were able to run for 167 minutes.

You want to feel energized going into a ride so you can get the most benefit from that time on the bike. You should eat a quick snack (the right sorts of preride snacks were listed in the nutrition chapter) and also make a point to drink water before you begin, especially if it's hot outside. Three cups of water is about right. If your body becomes dehydrated by as little as 2 percent, you can lose up to 10 percent in performance, because a lack of water actually makes it harder for your blood to deliver oxygen to your muscles.

Coffee provides a good preride pick-me-up and can improve endurance by mobilizing free fatty acids in the bloodstream. But don't count coffee as part of your daily water intake: The caffeine in coffee is a diuretic.

During your workout, the general rule of thumb is to drink before you feel thirsty, because you can lose up to 2 percent of your body weight as sweat or urine before your thirst mechanism sets in. Aim for a standard water bottle, or roughly 1 liter, each hour; more than that if it's hot outside. As for fuel, consume 300 to 500 calories, as either a sports drink or easily digestible food, for every hour of exercise. This is important: It keeps you riding strong, it keeps you in a positive mind-set (low blood sugar is associated with light-headedness), and you will recover more quickly for the next workout if you don't stress your body by forcing it to perform without adequate fuel.

After every ride, immediately drink at least 2 cups of water to rehydrate your body. And depending on how hard and how long you went, eat a carbohydrate-rich snack to replace the glycogen stores you likely used up during the session; that will help you recover more quickly so that you can come back in your next workout feeling great.

13 mph: Rest Hard, Play Hard

Sit in the slipstream of an elite-level cyclist—follow him or her around for a week—and you'll notice a few interesting things: First, they're quirky. They'll undergo their own strange machinations before workouts and competitions. Remember the movie *As Good as It Gets,* with Jack Nicholson, in which he'd obsessively lock and relock his front door? The best riders are notorious for doing stuff like that. They fidget with their gear and tinker with their bikes constantly.

Another interesting thing you'll discover is that elite riders take a lot of time *off* from their training. One day, you'll see them soaring full-throttle up a mountainside; the next, they'll do little or no training, they'll partake of a deep, hot bath, and they'll get to bed at an early hour. What's going on? They're recovering. *Seriously.*

In order to physically and emotionally withstand their backbreaking training regimes over time—and to continue to improve—elite athletes must allow their bodies time to repair. If they don't, they run the risk of burning out, plateauing, or sustaining chronic injuries. That's why successful athletes are as serious about their easy days as they are about their hard ones.

In fact, some believe that rest is the sine qua non of sports performance. "Recovery is the name of the game in sports," says Tour de France champion Lance Armstrong. "Whoever recovers the fastest does the best."

Armstrong's aphorism applies to you, too. The typical approach to getting fit is to work out as strenuously as possible, as often as possible; but that's simply not the best way to do it. It's ironic that one reason why people fail to achieve their fitness, weight-loss, or athletic goals is that they do too much too often.

By balancing the appropriate amounts of stress and rest in your workout program, you will minimize fatigue and your body will grow steadily stronger. Here's why.

When you work out—whether running, biking, or lifting weights— you break down a little muscle tissue. If you don't give that muscle a chance to rebuild, your body will remain in a perpetual state of disrepair. That's why, after weeks or months of consistent exercise, you can feel heavy legged or worn-out during workouts.

Some experts will tell you that it's during *periods of rest* that you actually grow fitter; the workouts simply provide the catalyst for the change. As glucose is dispersed into the bloodstream while you work out, your muscles use their own glycogen stores, along with the liver's, to fuel their work. Your body also uses water to fuel metabolic processes—and to cool off, in the form of sweat. So the harder or longer you ride, the more glycogen and water your body uses. If you conscientiously replenish those things after hard workouts—and take a couple of easy days to allow your body to properly resynthesize those things—you will come back to your next big ride stronger and more energized. If you don't, you can send yourself into an unremitting state of fatigue and depletion. This can cause a lack of motivation, a drop in athletic performance, and, over time, a state of severe exhaustion (known as chronic fatigue syndrome, or CFS), from which it can take months to recover.

The best approach is to challenge yourself one day, in terms of either workout duration or intensity, and then back off over the next couple of days. Do this, and you'll perform better on your hard days, leading to a better body and a supercharged sports performance.

Here's an interesting point: The process of recovery can actually begin during your workout. By properly nourishing and hydrating your body as you ride, you will recover more quickly, because you won't have over-stressed its resources during the workout. In other words, if you don't eat or drink during a long bike ride, it may take days for your body to reestablish its levels of hydration and glycogen. But drink 12 ounces of water and consume 200 to 300 calories an hour during exercise, and you'll be ready for more in 48 hours. That's one of the great secrets to better cycling and better fitness.

What's the best way to recover from hard cycling workouts? Some research has shown that active recovery can be more effective than complete rest. The idea is that by gently moving the body, blood will pump needed nutrients and oxygen to heal muscles and remove waste products that result from strenuous activity. Try going for an easy 20-minute swim or a relaxing 10-minute spin on your bike the day after a long, hard ride, and you will be amazed at how quickly you recover.

When you complete a series of stellar workouts followed by periods of well-deserved rest, your motivation grows, your confidence rises, and your cycling skyrockets. Take the "hard-easy-easy" approach over the next 10 weeks—and you'll begin to soar.

A great resource for learning more about how to maximize the benefits of your exercise by striking the ideal balance of stress and rest is *Optimal Muscle Performance and Recovery* by the late Edmund R. Burke, PhD, who was a nationally renowned exercise physiologist.

14 mph: Develop Your "Mental Muscle"

The inimitable Yogi Berra once said, "Baseball is 90 percent mental; the other half is in your head." While Berra was famous for such malapropisms, his quote underscores an important point: Your mind will help you immensely in your drive for 25.

However, in exercise and sports we tend to focus more on the muscles of our body while giving our "mental muscle" short shrift. By strengthening your mind, you can boost your cycling performance while enjoying your workouts more.

Sports psychology is the field of study that addresses the mental side of athletic performance. "Sports psychology essentially helps athletes of all levels develop the mental skills to maximize their competitive performances," says Jim Taylor, PhD, a sports psychologist and the author of *Prime Sport: Triumph of the Athlete Mind.*

There are four simple ways you can better your frame of mind as you ride your bike.

Focus More Narrowly

Experts agree that much of Tiger Woods's golfing greatness stems from his steely, unflappable focus. For example, in a trademark move, when Woods sets up for a putt, he kneels down, grabs the bill of his golf hat with both hands, and completely blurs out all external visual and auditory stimuli while zeroing in on one thing: the hole. Likewise, learning to zero in during your workouts can work wonders on your cycling performance.

"Begin by simply focusing on what you're doing on your bike," says Dr. Taylor. "For example, if you're riding on a stationary bike indoors, rather than read the paper, talk to friends, or watch TV, listen to inspiring music on a headset and tune in to your breathing, your heartbeat, and your pedaling technique. Focus on what your body is doing. That leads to better mental performance."

For most of us, distracting thoughts can cloud our minds during exercise. To combat this in your next workout, try to maintain a crystal-clear focus on what you're doing for as long as possible. You may start with a period of just 60 seconds, and that's fine. Over time, try to extend that mental focus to 5 minutes, 10 minutes, or even an entire workout. When you can ride for an hour and think of nothing but your breathing and your pedal motion, you will be amazed at the levels of performance that you can achieve.

Visualize Success

While mental imagery may at first sound like a New Age or ersatz technique, when used correctly, it can be a powerful tool to help you reach your cycling goal and perform better in life.

Effective visualization incorporates all five human senses: sight, sound, smell, touch, and taste. "In mental imagery, you attempt to reproduce the actual experience in your mind in as rich detail as possible," says Dr. Taylor.

Mental imagery serves a purpose similar to what rehearsals do for actors: It allows you to practice before the big performance, fortifying your confidence.

"All the research shows that mental imagery helps build confidence because people can literally 'see' themselves succeed—and that's important," says Dr. Taylor. "Some evidence also shows that imagery subtly triggers the muscles that people are visualizing, and physical skills can be developed because of that."

Here's how to do it: The night before an important workout, find a quiet place, close your eyes, relax your body, and for 5 to 10 minutes, picture yourself performing the way you want to perform. Visualize yourself riding with strength, ease, and grace, and tune in to how that feels.

Get Emotional

According to Dr. Taylor, there are five essential mental factors that most directly impact sports and exercise performance: motivation, confidence, intensity, focus, and emotion.

Lance Armstrong epitomizes what it means to use emotion to fuel higher levels of sports performance. When you observe Armstrong in particularly strenuous stages in the Tour, he's very focused, composed, and passionate. He lets his emotions well up inside of him and, much to the dismay of his competitors, completely unleashes those emotions into the pedals of his bicycle while maintaining virtually perfect pedaling technique. In other words, he doesn't smash down on the pedals when he rides hard; rather, he channels his emotion and his passion into *efficient* forward motion.

During your cycling workouts, stay focused on the positive, and tap into the power of your emotions to spur yourself on to greater heights.

Define Your Own Limits

Did you know that technically the bumblebee cannot fly? Scientists at NASA concluded after a series of tests and analyses that there is simply no way the bee can overcome its weight and body design to fly. Thankfully, the scientists didn't tell the bee, which flies about with a blissful disregard for humankind's most esteemed experts.

The indomitable bumblebee illustrates a key concept of exercise and sports performance: Much of the time, we allow others to define our limits and determine what we can and cannot do, and we set goals based on such external perceptions of ourselves. While it's important to lay out manageable exercise goals, it's also important to aim high once in a while. The act of setting a uniquely challenging goal serves as kind of a tacit show of faith in yourself—and that rallies your mind to the cause. "When we are striving to achieve a challenging goal, we say 'I'm going to set my mind to this,' not 'I'm going to set my body to this,' " says Dr. Taylor. We can achieve much more than we give ourselves credit for if we just set our minds to it.

If you experience a lull in your cycling program, recommit, in your mind, to the quest right now. Take a couple days off and refresh your legs. Then come back to your favorite ride the following day and get with a couple of friends—whatever it takes to make it fun and rewarding again.

15 mph: Ride with the Pack (at Least Once a Week)

Speaking of riding with others, to increase our motivation—and our skill level—we need to seek outside support. I cannot overemphasize how valuable it is for you to ride with experienced cyclists. You needn't pedal with the pros; there are thousands of group rides in almost every city around the country. Jump in. These rides attract people just like you, of all skill levels, and then break up into smaller groups as the ride progresses. Start with a group in which you feel comfortable, and keep challenging yourself to move up in the pack!

During these rides, ask the more experienced cyclists lots of questions. Take my word for it—we love to showcase our cycling acumen! Watch these riders corner and descend. Ask them about equipment issues you may have. These people have put in thousands of miles and have amassed an impressive amount of cycling wisdom.

One of the most striking visions of pack riding is the Tour de France, a great spectacle in the athletic world. The image of 150 cyclists pedaling along treacherous roads at 30 miles an hour, packed in shoulder to shoulder, is an impressive one.

You've likely seen the Tour on television: The peleton snakes through the French countryside, more closely resembling a single organism than a group of individual riders.

The average cyclist gazes in bewildered awe at how so many cyclists can ride so fast and so closely together. Others wonder why those riders prefer such close quarters!

The sport of cycling has a great deal to do with aerodynamics. Lance Armstrong nestles himself into that pack and always follows his teammates for one primary reason: to conserve his energy.

"When you ride close behind another bicyclist, you don't have to work as hard," said Dr. Burke. "The bicyclist in front of you serves as a windbreak, reducing your air resistance. Experienced bicyclists take advantage of this effect, drafting each other in a 'paceline,'" he said.

Now, take that benefit you derive from riding behind one cyclist and extrapolate it over a few dozen riders, as Lance Armstrong does in the Tour de France, and the effects are even more significant. A large group of riders forms a juggernaut that cuts the air and allows Armstrong to sail along on flat terrain without exerting much effort at all. That means he can ride just as fast while maintaining a heart rate much lower than when he rides alone. His teammates sacrifice themselves to preserve Armstrong in the early stages of the multistage Tour de France event by allowing him to draft behind them. "We don't want Lance to touch the wind until he has to," says former United States Postal Service (USPS) teammate Tyler Hamilton.

That's why you'll rarely see Lance Armstrong outside the protective shield of his loyal teammates. They not only cut the wind for Armstrong; they also pace, protect, and encourage him—and they even fetch his water! During one climb in the Tour de France, USPS coaches radioed to one of Armstrong's teammates, Christian Vande Velde, and explained that Armstrong needed water. Still far from the top of the mountain and in great physical pain himself, Vande Velde was ordered to turn around, ride downhill to the support vehicle, and race back uphill to hand the full water bottles off to Armstrong.

"There will be nights [after stages in the Tour de France] when Lance is fresh as a daisy, and all the support riders are facedown in their pasta, and that's the way it's supposed to be," says Frankie Andreu, USPS team director, an American who rode in nine Tours before retiring at the end of the 2000 season.

Nobody understands the value of teamwork more than Armstrong himself. "[Many people] don't understand that cycling is a *team* sport," says Armstrong. "They see a guy on a bike, they think: individual sport. At times it is. But I could never, ever win the Tour de France without the team. Never."

Of course, few of us will ride in events as grueling as the Tour de France against cyclists as menacing as Lance Armstrong, but we all can benefit from riding in packs—and it will help you achieve your goal of 25 miles an hour. Riding with others boosts your fitness, your coordination, and your composure under pressure, and it is one of the best ways to inject more fun into workouts. It's also safer, because a larger group of cyclists commands more respect from motorists, and, should an emergency or a bicycle malfunction arise, there are others around to help you.

Riding in a pack of cyclists, however, can be a daunting affair. Here are some tips that will maximize your enjoyment and your safety.

First, become eminently comfortable on your bike before you ride with a group. Hone the essential bike skills of cornering, climbing, shifting, and descending, to the point at which your bike feels like an extension of your body rather than a mass of metal beneath you. Once you capture that feeling, it's time to join the group.

The cardinal rule of pack riding is to remain calm. Cycling in a group is not nearly as dangerous as it appears. Think of it as driving in traffic: Most of the time, everyone moves along in a universally understood flow. People follow several unwritten rules that keep things safe and sane out there while driving. The same goes for pack cycling. It's only when someone hits that panic button and slams on their brakes that things go wrong. Keep your movements as smooth and predictable as possible.

Next, just as when you're driving in traffic, remain acutely aware of everything going on around you when cycling with others. When you drive your car, you don't fixate on the car in front of you; you constantly scan to the side and up several cars ahead. The same applies to cycling.

Every group ride takes on its own personality based on the skills and dispositions of its riders. Try to get a feel for the group dynamic early in the ride, and do your best to blend into the pace and rhythm.

Finally, cycle with others who know what they're doing out there. Seasoned cyclists ride more smoothly and can also give you valuable "on the bike" pointers.

Ultimately, as with most things, you learn best by doing. So put your fears, doubts, and self-imposed limits aside, put these strategies into action, and go ride with the pack!

Chapter Summary: Your Assignments

• Strive to get the greatest benefit from each bike ride by clearing your head of distracting thoughts; enjoying yourself fully; eating right before, during, and after the ride; and executing perfect pedaling technique as often as possible.

• Learn to breathe deeply and rhythmically on your bike and in daily life. Whenever it crosses your mind, stop and take a few full-body breaths to relieve stress. Also, use deep breathing to wash away pain during hard rides.

• Focus more on fueling yourself during cycling workouts. Your rides will feel easier, you'll perform better, and you'll recover faster.

• Assign as much focus and importance to rest days as you do to workouts, and tap the power of your mind by focusing more intensely during key workouts.

• Ride with a group of cyclists at least once a week, preferably on your hard key workout day.

OPENING UP THE THROTTLE: WEEKS 7 AND 8

There simply is no thrill quite like rocketing along on a bike fueled by the power of your own legs.

−Bernard Hinault, five-time Tour de France champion

You've been on the program now for 6 weeks. By now, you should be feeling a deeper connection to the bike and greater power in your heart, lungs, and legs. You are ready to introduce a very exciting element to your training: breakthrough workouts.

16 mph: Introduce Breakthrough Workouts

Most people ride at a moderate intensity throughout the week, which is sufficient for basic health maintenance; but if you're trying to lose those last few pounds or inject some serious performance and speed into your cycling, you must launch a new approach.

World-class athletes call them "key workouts" or "breakthrough sessions," the cornerstones of their training programs. Breakthrough sessions can provide you with exciting mental and physical results in a very short period of time. They can also increase your daily energy levels and prevent exercise-induced injury.

Why It Works

Before we get into the hows of breakthrough workouts, let's take a brief look at why this approach works from a physiological standpoint.

As you likely know, exercise like cycling places a positive stress on your body: By increasing the demands on your muscles and your cardiovascular system during a ride, your body responds by growing stronger and more efficient in preparation for the next workout.

"The human body is wonderfully adaptive," says George McGlynn, EdD, the author of *Dynamics of Fitness* and a former professor of exercise physiology at the University of San Francisco. "It directly responds to the quality and quantity of the exercise—or lack thereof—that you invest into it."

However, that same adaptability can also be our nemesis. Have you ever experienced a period in which, no matter how much you exercised or how little food you ate, your body didn't change proportionally? That is commonly known as a plateau, or a rut. What has happened is that your body has, in essence, gotten wise to you. Essentially, it's not being stressed sufficiently to change its shape or its level of performance. Exercise at 130 beats per minute ad infinitum, and your body will simply not dramatically respond.

That's where key workouts come in. They are designed to help you break through frustrating ruts and seemingly interminable plateaus.

Let me give you a personal example: In my first year as a triathlete, I achieved a good measure of success. I was working out only 4 hours a day, four times a week, but every one of those workouts was either very difficult or very long. They were very challenging, and my body and mind adapted to those increased demands. I was constantly improving, and my confidence grew as I reached new heights.

Then I made the classic rookie miscalculation: If 4 days a week led to a number-six world ranking, 7 days a week might give me a shot at a world title. I began training like a madman, 6 hours a day, every day of the week.

The result? I made no forward progress, because I was constantly fatigued. I had no energy to do those breakthrough sessions, and I never recovered from my workouts. I spent 2 years in an overtrained and exhausted state often fraught with nagging injuries.

Although you're not likely putting in those hours, the same rules of stress and rest apply to you.

How to Integrate Breakthrough Sessions into Your Cycling Program

A breakthrough session is generally defined as one that is either longer or more intense than you are accustomed to. If you are going to modify your program to include this sort of session, you must follow this simple but inviolable rule: Rest.

Performing breakthrough sessions requires a sharp mind and well-rested body. If you do a long bike ride, for example, you would take 2 or even 3 days completely off after that to allow your body to recover. Then, 3 days later, you would perform another breakthrough workout and rest again. This is how to get fit without fatigue and is the essence of smart training.

Get together. Have you ever noticed that when you're around other people during exercise, you tend to put in a little more effort? That's called social facilitation, and it's why breakthrough sessions are best performed with others. Group work-outs and even organized events will compel you to give that little extra effort that can produce extra-ordinary results.

Track your progress with benchmark rides. There is little that motivates us quite like seeing and feeling real results in our bodies. That is why experiencing a breakthrough workout can be so exhilarating. When you begin this new method of exercising, keep track of your sessions in a Success Journal (see page 42) so that you can gauge how well the new program is working. It is vital to measure your progress in what are called *heart-rate-to-time (or -distance) benchmarks*. This is simply the only way to determine your true aerobic fitness progress; anything else is mere guesswork.

For example, let's say a specific ride you do takes 45 minutes at an average heart rate of 140 beats per minute. Suddenly, you ride it in 39 minutes at the same average heart rate. This means your body has become roughly 13 percent more aerobically fit and efficient! That's exciting to see and naturally elevates your motivation. That is what breakthrough workouts are about—elevating your riding, your confidence, and your desire to ride.

Sample Breakthrough Workouts

Over-distance. If you've been doing 90 minutes for your long ride each week, you might want to consider picking a day on which you increase to 2½ hours. This will take some preparation and focus, but by pushing out of your comfort zone (in this case, in terms of distance, not intensity), you will become a much stronger cyclist. Your RPE for over-distance rides should hover between 10 and 14. You never want to feel like you're riding hard during these rides. The goal here is to build endurance at a nice, steady pace for a longer period of time.

Super-sprints. It's week 7 and your body can handle more intense workouts now. Why not open things up and give it everything you've got in your next interval session? Here's a sample workout: Perform this session on a safe, flat road free from traffic or on an indoor trainer. After a long warmup, unleash five 20-second sprints at 95 percent of your maximum effort. These super-sprints will work wonders on developing your high-end speed and power on the bike.

Apply the simple but very useful maxim *work hard, play hard* to your cycling program, and you will experience steadier long-term progress. You will also see what you're really made of during rides—and that is the most exciting and rewarding part of breaking through to new levels of performance.

17 mph: Train Smart, Not Hard

It may be the biggest—and most dangerous—mistake that novice cyclists make. It can lead to unnecessary pain and nagging injuries, and in some cases, it can even cause a general meltdown and put an end to one's cycling program. It's the notion that to achieve results and to excel in cycling, you must ride hard all the time.

You may be thinking: "Wait a minute. Don't I have to really push myself in order to ride 25 miles an hour?" Yes, there are times when you must push your body (such as in breakthrough workouts). But the notion of hammering on the pedals in every ride is counterproductive in the long run.

The "harder is better" work ethic is revered in our culture, but it is one of the most prevalent and potentially hazardous exercise myths in America. Studies have shown that the body responds to exercise best when stressed at a moderately intense level during a week interspersed with one or two hard or long workouts. Isn't it nice to know you can slow down and get better results?

An effective way to visualize this notion of smarter cycling is to picture a cost-benefit graph: As you increase your pace, the health and fitness benefits rise, but only to a point. After that, you reap only marginal results, but your fatigue levels and risk of injury begin to rise exponentially. The trick is to increase your cycling effort to that ideal point. Usually, that effort level doesn't require a pace as frenetic as most people believe.

Riding in your ideal zone is important across all sports, but it's particularly crucial when engaging in strenuous sports such as cycling, because riding can be an exhausting activity. "Whatever your cycling goal, you will get there easier and more efficiently if you run in your optimal zones," says Sally Edwards, an exercise specialist and the author of *The Heart Rate Monitor Guidebook to Heart Zone Training*. "Each of us is different and we must find our own 'ideal cycling zone,'" she advises.

(*Continued on page 104*)

How to Make Better Diet and Exercise Choices Each Day

Make healthy choices before your head can talk you out of them, and you'll find the inspiration needed to achieve fitness success. It's one of the fundamental tenets of human physiology: How well you eat and exercise directly impacts how good you look, feel, and think. Most of us accept that truth, yet we still find ourselves struggling to make the best diet and workout choices. Sugar cravings, lack of time, and exercise ennui are well-known barriers to better fitness, but your biggest nemesis may be your own mind. "When you make a poor diet or exercise choice, it's much more mental than physical," says Jim Taylor, PhD, a sports psychologist and the author of *Prime Sport: Triumph of the Athlete Mind.* "It's not that you're too tired to work out; it's that you *convince* yourself that you are."

Case in point: the preworkout internal debate in which you teeter between riding and packing it in. You may feel tired when you begin, but once you get rolling, you get energized; it's a matter of overcoming that initial mental hurdle. The same goes for eating well: You know the triple chocolate decadence may not be the wisest choice, but you order up anyway. If you find yourself rummaging for the remote control instead of your cycling shoes or reaching for the baklava instead of the banana, the trick is to interrupt those negative mental patterns by taking positive actions that get you on the right track before you can think not to be. Here's how.

Cue Yourself In

"Different visual and auditory cues can be very powerful motivators," says Dr. Taylor. "What we see and hear can influence our moods—and the decisions we make." For example, watching a televised cycling event may inspire you to get up and go for a bike ride. Even smaller cues, like having your workout gear and healthy food at your fingertips or posting inspiring pictures of athletes and fit bodies, motivational quotes, and other words of encouragement, will keep your mind on making healthy choices.

On a series of index cards, write down your best excuses for skipping workouts on the front ("I'm exhausted"; "It's cold outside"). On the back, counter them with fresh, compelling reasons to do the workout ("Exercise energizes me"; "Have fun—try a new workout today"). You can do the same thing with diet excuses and solutions, as well as posting inspirational quotes and pictures in places you'll see most.

Act Before You Think

"Our ability to rationalize and reason can be our downfall," says Diane Roberts Stoler, EdD, a licensed psychologist in Georgetown, Massachusetts, who is board certified in both health and sports psychology and is a member of the American Psychological Association. "We can list a dozen reasons why we shouldn't work out or why we 'deserve' the candy bar. Much of the time, we give in to those reasons." But if you do something before the thought processes start, your head will likely follow your body's lead. "Most of the time, it's just a matter of getting started down the right path," says Dr. Stoler.

When the time to get out for a ride is approaching, clear your head of any thoughts and simply take action; begin getting dressed for your workout. Your mind won't even have a chance to steer you in another direction once you get going.

Look to the Future

If you *do* start to entertain the idea of skipping your workout, don't stop there. Allowing your thoughts to roll all the way through until you can clearly picture what the end result will be may help you make a healthier choice. "The clearer you can visualize the consequences of your actions, the better chance you'll have making the right decisions," says Dr. Taylor.

The next time you face a tough diet or workout choice, take a moment to tune in to how you will feel moments after making your decision—visualize the consequences of both the bad choice and the good one. For example, as you start thinking about ordering the fried calamari, lasagna, and cannoli, feel your stomach distend, and even picture the extra fat on your frame. Next, see yourself starting with a salad, followed by the chicken piccata, and envision yourself looking lean and sated instead of stuffed and sick.

(Continued)

> (*Cont.*)
> **Delay the Temptations**
> Of course you can indulge every now and then, and you can take a break from exercise, but taking those moments off your program as a reward for doing something good may be the best way to trick your mind into staying on track.
> Make it a rule that you'll allow yourself only 3 days off in a row after you've completed a couple weeks of consistent exercise, and allow yourself an indulgent treat only after you've eaten something good for you. If you always do something healthy *before* something less healthy, the latter may lose its appeal altogether.

The best cycling zone for most people is between 70 and 90 percent of their aerobic maximum. If you want to ride strong for many years, you should exceed that number only during your interval or tempo cycling workouts.

A note to more competitive cyclists: Indeed, it's important to push to your aerobic maximum and beyond, but keep in mind that physiologically, regardless of your fitness level or goals, you will get the best possible results from building your aerobic engine, and that happens when you ride aerobically, below your maximum. If you seek a performance gain, you need to do only one anaerobic or hard ride per week. Any more than that and you risk injury and performance plateaus, because your body enters a state of ongoing exhaustion.

One of the best ways to gauge your effort—and ride at your own ideal intensity level—is to use a heart rate monitor in combination with the RPE scale. You will get the most out of your cycling when you ride at an RPE between 12 and 16. In this zone, you are pushing your body and positively stressing it without causing undue fatigue.

Begin to judge your rides on heart rate and RPE, and you will go a long way to zeroing in on the best cycling intensity for your body. You'll likely find that it's a lot slower than you've been cycling recently. And in most cases, slowing down is a good thing.

18 mph: Get Slick

As you start moving faster on the bike, your biggest resistance isn't your lack of fitness; it's the air. Did you know that roughly 75 percent of your energy goes to overcoming wind resistance when you ride 18 to 22 miles an hour? The relationship between wind resistance and speed is a logarithmic one: The faster you go, the more the resistance pushes back on you. That's why you'll see riders in the Tour de France trying to get as low, narrow, and slick as possible during the time trials. The wind is their biggest nemesis.

As you start riding faster, you need to think about slicing through the air like a hot knife through butter rather than mashing through it like a Mack truck.

Watch top professional cyclists. Everything is designed to reduce their frontal drag (susceptibility to wind resistance). Their bodies are posi-

tioned lower on the bike; their arms are pulled in a little tighter; they pedal with their legs tucked in tight against the bike rather than flailing out with bowed knees. The key is to get comfortable in those slicker positions.

Once you have the right bike, it's time to make some basic adjustments to get into a position that presents a little less frontal drag. Over the next few weeks, strive to get your body into a more compact position on the bike: Lower your handlebars a little. Start to bring those elbows

Bike to Work

Commuting to work on your bike is a great way to boost your fitness, increase your mental clarity, lose weight, reduce stress, save time and money, and spare the environment—not to mention train for your triathlon! When the weather allows, give it a try. It's a way to sneak in training time that just may change your life. It did mine. When I first thought about biking to work, I had all the typical doubts: I didn't have enough time. It was too much hassle. I was still too out of shape. All of those reservations vanished after the first week.

Take the time issue, for instance: When I began my bike commute, riding 45 minutes to and from work 3 days a week, I didn't need additional cycling workouts! And once I streamlined my routine, which took only four or five rides, biking to work became not a hassle but an essential part of my day.

Here's how I streamlined my routine.

First, I'd gather all of my gear and clothing for work the night before. Next, I'd make sure my bike was in good working order so that I didn't have to make any repairs or adjustments during the commute. Finally, I would explore different routes and map out the ideal route to ensure that I got to work efficiently and that I encountered the least vehicular traffic.

The ride cleared my head and mentally centered me for a more productive workday. It helped control my appetite all day, inspiring me to

in. Angle your torso a little more aggressively rather than sitting perfectly upright. Remain cognizant of getting slick, and your body will naturally start to move into the optimal position.

19 mph: Get Present

Better cycling performance can be found in the moment. On a recent 4-hour bicycle ride with a group of professional cyclists, I was approaching my physical, emotional, and spiritual limits. I'm a triathlete, and these cycling specialists were climbing mountains faster than I had ever climbed before—and descending even faster, reaching speeds up to make better food choices. I was less inclined to eat an extra-large piece of cheese pizza when I knew I'd have to drag it up that hill on the way home.

That's another benefit of cycling to work: It requires you to ride home! The evening commute aids in the digestion of the food eaten during the day and creates a healthy appetite for your evening meal.

Last but not least, it relieves work-related stress. Cycling has a way of putting life into perspective. It's satisfying to watch a traffic jam while you stream past on your bike, your legs pumping, your body fully alive. I guarantee that the argument with your co-worker will seem far less earth-shattering after your ride home. These reasons are why I fell in love with cycling and what eventually led me to become a professional triathlete. The bike made me stronger, healthier, and happier.

Plus, bicycle commuting is easier than you think. It just takes some intelligent planning and a willingness to break out of your rut. Besides your regular bike gear, the only stuff you'll need is a lock and a well-fitting backpack to hold your work clothes and toiletries.

Remember to go easy for the last 10 minutes of each ride to cool your body temperature. I made the rookie bike-commuting mistake of riding hard all the way to work. I became so superheated that for the first hour at my desk, I sweated like a farm animal. Take my word for it: You don't want your cubicle smelling like a pigsty!

60 miles per hour. My mind was scattered; I was having trouble staying in the moment.

Then, it happened.

I heard a mash of twisted metal behind me and turned to see a pile of cyclists who had crashed and careened off the road. Amazingly, everyone was okay, except for a few cases of road rash and bruised egos. When I asked one of the riders how the crash had happened, he said, "I caused the accident. I lost my focus. My mind was preoccupied on catching the riders ahead of me, and my bike slid out from under me."

While you will likely never push to that kind of limit, this incident highlights an important point for anyone who exercises: Staying more fully present in each moment during workouts will increase safety and reduce your risk of injury. It can also boost performance and help you enjoy physical activity more.

Let's cover safety first. By paying more attention to your immediate surroundings during outdoor exercise, you reduce your risk of mishaps. For example, if you resolutely maintain your focus during every moment you're on a bicycle, you will naturally be more sensitized to everything around you—including the errant car that might dart out ahead of you. It's when your mind begins to wander that you risk getting into trouble.

The same goes for exercise-induced injuries. According to the American College of Sports Medicine, almost half of all injuries during physical activity occur when people are not paying attention to their bodies. By staying alert during exercise, you will be able to address potential problems—such as sensing tight hamstrings and stopping to stretch them—before they progress to the point of injury.

Awareness during exercise can also take your performance to the next level. Top performers in music, art, and sports focus all of their attention on the process. They become deeply immersed in giving their best in each moment, and in doing so, they create a performance that is a string of their best moments. That's how they achieve such remarkable results.

You can achieve this focus, too, and it can lead to a mental state known as *flow,* an experience that Mihaly Csikszentmihalyi presents in his book *Flow: The Psychology of Optimal Experience* as one of the most profound experiences a person can have. Scientists have shown that when in this state, the brain produces alpha waves, which are associated with relaxation and intense focus. By staying present in your body during exercise, you can tap into an inner strength and string together a series of your best moments—which lead to more effective and beneficial workouts.

Picture yourself conducting two different bike rides: In the first session, you bolt out the door with no warmup and allow yourself to be preoccupied with work-related stress—all the while staring down at the pavement. In the second, you roll outside first thing in the morning, take several deep breaths, shake out your body, and ease into the ride. You focus on the cool morning air, the smell of summer, your breathing, your fluid pedaling cadence, and your heartbeat. You keep your mind clear, and you look around to see things you haven't seen before.

While the second bike ride may sound Pollyannaish, it's this slowing down and staying in the moment that can transform otherwise bland workouts into richly rewarding, more timeless experiences.

Action Item

Pick one ride each week in which you try to remain entirely present in each moment. This skill is best cultivated during a solitary workout in a beautiful spot. When you are in this place—mind quiet, senses fully alive—time will fall away, and you will open up to new physical experiences and higher mental performances. This is precisely what the best athletes feel when they set world records.

Once you master present-moment awareness during your cycling, begin applying it to other areas of your life. It will put you in greater control and turn ordinary moments into extraordinary experiences.

20 mph: Make Cycling a Family Affair

Right about now, you're probably becoming an inspiration to your entire family. They're realizing that this isn't a passing phase for you, that you're not some flash in the pan. You're simply not giving up! This kind of resolute dedication will naturally inspire those around you to take up exercise in their individual quests to live better lives. This is one of the most wonderful fringe benefits of committing to living a healthier life; it spurs others to follow suit. And perhaps the most important people to get hooked on cycling are your kids. Children have never before needed more fitness guidance, and parents are the best people to provide it.

The National Center for Health Statistics shows that nearly 6 million children in the United States between the ages of 6 and 17 are "severely overweight." That number is more than double what it was in the 1970s. A recent report by the *Journal of American Medicine* found that the rates of child obesity in this country are rising due to record low levels of physical activity. According to this study, the average American child now exercises less than 1 hour per week.

This threatens the long-term health of our youth: The overweight children of today are most likely to become tomorrow's obese adults, placing themselves at risk for a variety of health problems, including high blood pressure, heart attacks, and diabetes.

Meanwhile, parents are busier than ever and have less time to exercise. Roughly 77 million adults in America do no physical activity at all, which contributes to the more than 300,000 premature deaths from conditions related to obesity.

That's the bad news. Here's the good news: These two serious and pervasive problems can be improved simultaneously with one simple strategy—ride your bike with your children more often.

"Integrating family and fitness is probably the single most effective way to boost your children's health *and* liberate more exercise time for you," says Steve Bennett, coauthor of the best-selling book *365 TV-Free Activities You Can Do with Your Child.* "Adjust your attitude and your approach just a little, and time spent exercising with your children can also be a lot of fun," he says.

How much time? Most experts agree that four 30-minute sessions per week are ideal.

Think outside the Box

The first step is to rewire your perceptions about exercise. Any physical activity you do with your children is beneficial. If your heart rate is between 100 and 150 beats per minute, you build cardiovascular fitness, whether you ride alone on trails or even with your kids! The next time you ride with your children, tap into their innate sense of play and adventure. If your boy or girl is competitive, then race them to various landmarks on your ride. If they are more about enjoying the scenery, then take them on longer adventures to seek out new landscapes. Understand what drives your child, and then use your bikes to thrill them. The point here is to think outside the box in terms of what activities to do: Ask your kids where they'd like to ride that week, and follow their lead right out the door. Just make sure it's a high-energy activity—and you must take part!

Make It a Regular Part of Your Life

Whether you think you have time for it or not, riding with your children will help them gain confidence and increase their chances of growing into healthier adults. It can also infuse you with a childlike sense of passion for the bike. These are two huge payoffs. According to Bennett, parents must "make a serious commitment to include actual, physical time in their busy schedules for long walks, bicycle riding, and physical activity that the whole family can enjoy."

It might surprise you, but kids themselves seem to agree. A recent survey conducted by the Gallup organization found that three out of five kids who exercise regularly said they do so because their parents and family encourage them to do so.

Make Fun the Focus

One reason why children may avoid exercise is that it's not as much fun as it could be: Coaches at school, overzealous parents, and a culture that places an "all-or-nothing" premium on winning engender performance anxieties in our children.

Experts say that if you tell your kids to go exercise, they are less likely to do it than if you package the request more attractively with a "let's go play on the bikes" instead. We all want our children to grow into healthy adults, and for that to happen, kids must develop positive associations with physical activity early, which begins with having as much fun as possible.

I am living proof of this. The only reason I can happily train 30 hours a week as a professional athlete is that my mom always made sure I had fun with sports as a kid. While she encouraged me to try new things, she never expected me to *perform*. A priceless gift, indeed.

Establish New Rituals

Most American rituals and holidays revolve around food: Thanksgiving *dinner,* Easter *chocolate,* birthday *cake,* Christmas . . . *everything.*

But integrating fun physical activities into family gatherings may reap big rewards, according to Sharon Lambton, RN, a pediatric nurse consultant for the California Department of Health Services. "Little things like going on a 'turkey trot' before Thanksgiving dinner can do wonders for the mental and physical health of all generations in attendance," Lambton suggests.

Television viewing is another omnipresent American ritual. How about challenging your kids to earn their TV time? If they can beat you in a bike race around the block, they get to watch television for an hour. Sounds corny, but it could produce positive results: Maybe you end up racing two out of three. Maybe you never make it back to the TV. Again, think outside the box.

Let Your Children Guide You

Physical activity comes more naturally to children than it does to us. For them, the sheer act of riding a bike is the fun part. Somewhere along the way, we lost sight of how exhilarating exercise can be—perhaps that's why we avoid it so steadfastly.

Our children can teach us a lot about getting back into our bodies, living in the moment, and having fun on the bike. Did you know that the average child laughs 300 times a day? The average adult? Only 20.

Enriching our physical and mental health and that of our children comes down to our ability to think and play like kids again. Get outside with an open mind and an open heart, and ride with your children. Do that, and you will reap the rich rewards that come from making cycling a family affair: You will enhance your cycling performance in your drive for 25 while improving the lives of your children.

BREAKING THROUGH TO THE OTHER SIDE: WEEKS 9 AND 10

There is only one real failure in life that is possible, and that is not to be true to the best we know.

—Frederic Farrar, American writer and educator

Congratulations. You're steaming down the homestretch—and you're flying! Welcome to the final and most exciting 2 weeks of your cycling program. You've put in the time and the miles. Now it's time to cash in on that investment and feel the thrill that comes from soaring on your bike and reaching your goal of that rarefied speed of 25 miles per hour.

Sometimes we forget what we're truly capable of. We tend to scale back our goals as we get older. But this quest has been largely about learning how much you really have in you. Now it's about breaking through—and riding right over—all of your fears, doubts, setbacks, and excuses.

115

21 mph: Roll over the Setbacks

When you go out on a limb to achieve a lofty goal, the potential payoffs are great, but so are the risks. Over the past few weeks, you've been pushing your body hard—moving further out onto that limb—and you will ramp things up yet again over the next two.

Things may start to get tough here. Whatever happens, don't get derailed. Obstacles, detours, and mistakes are all part of any serious and successful training program. Here's how to use the tough times to your advantage and even inspire yourself to greater heights on the bike.

You needn't be a conspiracy theorist to feel like there are plots at work to keep you from riding! You might do everything you can to get out on the bike, but there are days when everything and everyone—from your demanding boss to the mass of drivers in rush-hour traffic to the pint of ice cream in the freezer—get in your way! And what of those setbacks beyond your control—the inclement weather, the nagging pain, the limited hours in every day?

Obstacles are part of the natural order in fitness. It's not whether you experience them in your cycling program—we all do—*it's what you do with them that matters*. People who learn to leverage setbacks to their advantage enjoy greater success in fitness and in life.

"We learn more when we fail than when we succeed, because succeeding doesn't force introspection the way failing does," says Sherri McMillan, co-owner of Northwest Personal Training and Fitness Education in Vancouver, Washington. "Making mistakes or experiencing failures is a good thing. They can teach you a lot about how to improve your exercise program and your life."

Here are a few strategies for not only moving beyond the obstacles but emerging stronger, more confident, and better on the bike because of them.

• Air things out. Avoiding problems in your cycling program, such as a lingering injury or chronic fatigue, is like ignoring your finances and wondering why you're losing money. It only gets worse. Identify what's really going on, and write down your findings to develop the road map to improve things. "Seeing problems on paper begins the creative process of resolving them," says McMillan.

• Identify the roots of your weaknesses in your cycling program, and use that information to fortify your resolve and improve your performance. Think back to past mistakes or problems, and write down three to five possible ways to resolve each one. If knee pain has plagued you, your list may read: (1) Schedule an appointment with a knee specialist; (2) get a proper bike fitting; (3) avoid the hills for a while.

Sometimes collaborating with a friend who is experiencing similar setbacks can net better results.

• Free yourself from perfectionism. In fitness, an all-or-nothing mentality can lead to frustration and declining motivation. "Striving for perfection is what leads to failure," says McMillan. "The trick is learning to compromise. If you don't have a full hour to ride, just go for 30 minutes, or even 15. When it comes to exercise, any activity is better than none." When you experience an off day in your cycling, don't skip the entire session—just get out there and make an adventure of it. Often our most magical workouts come when we don't overthink them.

• Accept the process in its entirety. In these 10 weeks, you will experience highs and lows; that's just part of the deal. "The human body goes through distinct physiological changes over the course of each month, often referred to as circatrigintan rhythms," says Murray Mittleman, MD, assistant professor in the department of epidemiology at Harvard University School of Public Health and a board member of the American Association of Medical Chronobiology and Chronotherapeutics. "These physical highs and lows are perfectly natural. Relative to exercising, the best thing to do is listen to your body and modify your fitness program accordingly, even day to day."

When you're experiencing a low in your cycling program, work *with* your body, not against it. Take some time off. Get a massage. Regain your perspective. During that downtime, make a list of everything you will do when you're feeling better, and commit to coming back to things stronger, more confident, and more resilient. Then *do it.*

The Healing Touch of Bodywork

Sometimes you just feel so worn-out that nothing seems to help energize you. If this sounds familiar, you may want to consider getting some "work"—bodywork, that is. In 1 hour, you can feel completely reenergized both physically and mentally.

Do you remember the classic *Seinfeld* episode in which Jerry was dating that professional masseuse to get free bodywork—but he could never quite score it? That's me. I'm always trying to wheedle my way into my wife's hands for a free rubdown. Never works.

Here's a recipe for total relaxation: Partake of a deep soak and follow it with a full-hour massage—and you're a new you. Normally, when we finish getting professional bodywork, we think, "I *have* to do that more often!" We don't realize how out of whack are bodies are until we get rubbed. The fact is, you will be placing great demands on your body over the next 2 weeks. If you've ever deserved a massage, now is the time.

Professional bodywork relaxes your muscles, soothes your mind, and gives you an enhanced sense of well-being. But the benefits run deeper than that: Science has shown that bodywork can help to heal existing muscular injuries, reduce the risk of future injury, and even improve your performance in exercise and your daily life.

Elite athletes covet massage and get it up to six times per week to function at their peak. But for most people, bodywork is a luxury they simply cannot afford. Hourly rates can be upward of $80. (There are inexpensive alternatives, which I've outlined below.)

As more research surfaces about the healing benefits of bodywork, some experts believe that this form of therapy is something we cannot afford to do without, particularly as our bodies are subjected to the increasing stresses of daily life.

"Years of improper stretching, driving, sitting, standing, walking, carrying groceries, talking on the telephone, working at the computer . . . lead to pain, injury, and general discomfort," says Andrew Weil, MD, author and internationally acclaimed health expert. "Indeed, many of us have forgotten how good our bodies can feel until we get expert bodywork," he says.

You are pushing your body hard, and you should regard a bodywork expense much like a utility bill to maintain your most prized possession. Each month you devotedly pay your water bill, your energy bill, and your cable bill. Why not your "body bill"? After all, you are logging the miles on the bike. You deserve and need it.

Here is an overview of the most popular and effective forms of bodywork and important considerations for each.

Regular Massage

This is the most popular variety of bodywork. It varies from a nice, gentle, invigorating rubdown to what is known as deep-tissue massage, geared to more serious sports enthusiasts.

The primary benefit of massage is that it almost invariably washes away your mental and physical stress and leaves you feeling relaxed and refreshed. Another benefit of getting massage from experts is that they can check over your body and ferret out injuries before they occur. In other words, they might find that your hamstring is tightening up (perhaps your saddle is too high), and by working on that area, they help you avoid an injury to your hamstring later on. That's invaluable.

A good massage therapist will ask you lots of questions about your body and focus on those areas that are either causing you pain or not functioning properly. Make sure that the therapist works on the primary movers involved in cycling: your quadriceps, gluteals, hamstrings, lower back, and calves.

Low-Cost Option: There are massage schools across the country. The students need a requisite number of hours for certification. I've found that they often do a better job than the seasoned pros, because they try harder. That means a better massage for you for less money. (Remember that massage therapy may be covered by your health insurance. Indeed, not all insurers provide this coverage, but it may be worth doing some research to find a plan that does.)

Rolfing

Rolfing is massage on caffeine, and it's great for more serious cyclists. Rolfing is a very deep massage developed by Ida P. Rolf (1896–1979), PhD, a biochemist and therapist. Dr. Rolf claimed she found a correlation between muscular tension and pent-up emotions.

(Continued)

(Cont.)

Rolfing is generally intended to restructure the connective tissue and typically consists of 10 intensive sessions in which the practitioner applies firm—even slightly painful—pressure with the fingers and elbows to specific parts of the body.

This form of bodywork is best for people with chronic injuries or long-standing problems of bad posture and chronic discomfort (such as back pain). It can also help diminish habitual muscle tension; many professional cyclists swear by rolfing.

Low-Cost Option: Contact the Rolf Institute at (800) 530-8875, and they can lead you to a rolfing expert in your area and your price range.

Acupuncture

This form of bodywork is over 5,000 years old. Shen Nung, the father of Chinese medicine, documented theories about circulation, pulse, and the heart more than 4,000 years before European medicine even began exploring these areas. His insights led to the development of modern acupuncture. Acupuncture is the insertion of very fine needles on the body's surface in order to influence its physiology.

As the basis of acupuncture, Nung theorized that the body had an energy force running throughout it. This energy force is known as *chi* (pronounced "chee"). The chi consists of all essential activities, which include the spiritual, emotional, mental, and physical aspects of life. A person's health was therefore thought to be influenced by the flow of chi in the body.

While this may appear closer to astrology than astronomy to most of you, acupuncture has given millions of people serious relief. In addition, the National Institutes of Health reported that "there is clear evidence" that acupuncture is "an acceptable alternative" to conventional treatments for stroke rehabilitation, headache, menstrual cramps, tennis elbow, fibromyalgia, lower-back pain, carpal tunnel syndrome, and asthma.

Low-Cost Option: There are none. Acupuncture is best left to certified experts. Never attempt to do acupuncture on yourself or others.

Chiropractic

This form of bodywork has long been stigmatized, but it's becoming more mainstream as access to a higher quality of chiropractors increases. According to the American Chiropractic Association, "the practice and procedures of chiropractic specifically include the adjustment and manipulation of the articulations and adjacent tissues of the human body, particularly of the spinal column."

Good chiropractic care can be stellar, but bad treatments can be atrocious. That is why it's imperative for you to ensure your practitioner is a highly respected, certified, experienced chiropractor before you let him or her anywhere near your neck.

After getting chiropractic treatments around the world, I've learned one universal truth: Your chiropractor should do muscle-tissue work around your neck and back before he or she adjusts those areas, because if your muscles are tight and your spine is adjusted, those tight muscles will simply pull your spine right back out of alignment.

Low-Cost Option: There are none. Chiropractic work is best left to certified experts. Never attempt to do chiropractic on yourself or others.

Whatever bodywork you decide to get, follow these important tips.

• Fully relax during your bodywork. The more you can calm your mind and your muscles, the more benefit you will get from the session. Focus on breathing deeply and clearing your mind.

• Because bodywork can be an intimate experience for some people, choose someone with whom you feel implicitly comfortable.

• Don't ride hard directly after bodywork. Allow the effects of the massage to sink in all day. You can hammer the pedals the day after your massage; it will probably be one of your best rides!

• You know your body better than any massage therapist. If something doesn't feel right, stop. Communication with the person working on you is paramount.

Your body is the most wondrous piece of machinery you will ever own. Treat it as such. Get at least two tune-ups over the next 14 days; you will feel and perform better in your cycling workouts and in your daily life.

22 mph: Enter a Bike Race

Every year in June, one of the great athletic spectacles circumnavigates France at a fearsome rate. The Tour de France is the world's preeminent cycling event, in which nearly 200 top-echelon riders cut a vibrant, multicolored swath through the French countryside and cover an astonishing 2,000-plus miles in just 22 days.

While watching the event on television is awe inspiring, getting out there and saddling up for a bike race yourself is flat-out awesome.

You needn't pedal like Lance Armstrong to participate in a cycling event. Whether you're a novice, a weekend warrior, or a serious cyclist, now is the time to enter a competitive bike race. It's not as hard as it looks, and training for the event will make you as fit as you've ever been. The actual event will be one of the most thrilling experiences of your life. There is no question that training for and participating in an organized cycling race will help you achieve your goal of 25 miles an hour.

Pre-Event Checklist

The most daunting element of road racing may be the general anxiety people feel prior to the event. As with anything else, thorough preparation can attenuate most of those fears.

• Join a bike club. Riding with others will teach you more about road racing than anything else. Ride with a group at least once a week, and ask the more experienced riders lots of questions.

• Pick your event. Assess your current fitness level and your goals. Then choose an event that is well organized and plays to your strengths. For example, if you are a "mountain goat" (a strong climber), pick a race packed with hills.

• Review the course. Try to either ride or drive the course prior to event day. Often, what we fear most is the unknown. Having a good look at the course will boost your race-day performance and your safety, since you'll know what to expect.

Training

The best way to approach any athletic event is to become familiar with the specific physical demands of that event. For example, if your bike race has lots of corners and climbs in it, you should spend extra time honing these two skills in training. Also, bike racing requires you to ride at many different speeds, so you will need to train your body to develop endurance, strength, and speed.

Race Tips

• Eat a light, bland, carbohydrate-rich meal at least 2 hours before the event. This will top off your energy stores without upsetting your stomach.

• Arrive early. If this is your first race, it will take you longer than you can imagine to prepare for the event. Regardless of how many bike races I do, I find myself rushing like a madman to the start line of each one.

• Though it may seem counterintuitive, the shorter your event, the more time you need to warm up for it. That's because races, such as criteriums—you know, those wild-paced events that race around a city block multiple times, for example—are generally ridden at much faster paces, and your body needs to be ready to go hard right from the start.

• Arrive at the starting line at least 5 minutes before the race is scheduled to begin. Try to stay loose, do some last-minute stretching, and remain calm. Reflect on all of your training.

• Moments before the start, take three very deep breaths, clear your mind, and say to yourself, "Stay present in each moment, give your best every step of the way, and *have fun!*"

• As a triathlete, I have trouble following the cardinal rule of bike racing: Conserve your energy. In a triathlon, you are not allowed to draft another rider; in bike racing, that's the smartest strategy. It saves a lot of energy. The wind is your enemy, so stay out of it.

• As for nutrition, if the race lasts less than an hour, plain water will suffice. For events longer than that, you will need to consume 200 to 500 calories an hour. To find what works best for you, explore different foods and sports drinks during training.

• As much as possible, try to spend most of your race in the top third of the pack. You will evade most of the crashes that way. You will also avoid what is known as "the accordion effect," in which the pack expands and contracts due to the constantly changing speeds within the group. If you're near the front, you don't feel the changes as much.

Finally, seize the race day. In your bike event—just as in the event of life—be true to your best.

23 mph: Fend Off Sports Injuries

While cycling is a sport with a relatively low risk of injury (barring acute events like crashes), you should still know how to recognize and treat injuries before they become nagging, chronic conditions.

Research shows that people ride more in summer than in fall, spring, and winter combined. While this increased summertime physical activity benefits you in many ways—improved cardiovascular health, reduced risk of disease, increased ability to eat more chocolate guilt-free—it can also lead to aches and pains. A pulled hamstring muscle from a hard ride and a lower-back strain from lifting weights are prime examples.

According to the *Merck Manual of Medical Information for Sports Injuries,* Americans suffer more than 10 million sports injuries each year. Surprisingly, despite this widespread prevalence of exercise-induced injuries and the mental and physical suffering they can inflict, few people actually know what's wrong with their bodies, and even fewer know how to treat their pain effectively.

For example, let's say you pull a muscle in your back while on a ride. You might stretch and apply a heat pack to the area, since that feels like the right thing to do. But the reality is that stretching and heating a muscle pull in the first 72 hours will reinflame the affected muscle and can actually worsen the condition.

To minimize the negative effects of injuries, you must first understand exactly what kind of injury you have, and then apply the appropriate treatment early. In fact, what you do over the first 72 hours of a soft-tissue injury will do more to determine its duration and severity than what you do over the subsequent 4 weeks.

There are lots of types of sports injuries, but we'll stick to the two most common: muscle *sprains* and muscle *strains*.

Let's begin with a little anatomy lesson so that you can better understand how and why injuries occur. There are three primary reasons why you get injured during exercise.

The most common cause of soft-tissue injury is overuse. Working a muscle or tendon until it's no longer capable of handling the workload can cause that area to pull or tear. Continuing to exercise after that point only exacerbates the injury.

Next, because everyone is built differently, some of us are more prone, or *biomechanically predisposed,* to injuries as a result of engaging in certain sports than in others. You likely instinctually know which sports you're cut out for and which ones you should avoid. For example, if you have a heavier frame, you may enjoy and perform better at cycling than running, which is a high-impact, weight-bearing activity.

Finally, muscles, tendons, and ligaments may become injured as a result of weakness. If you push a weak muscle too hard, it will give, in the form of a sprain or strain.

Let's look at those two types of injuries and what you should do to treat them.

A *sprain* is an injury to a ligament—the tough, fibrous tissue that connects your bones or cartilages at a joint. The severity of a sprain will depend on the extent of injury to a single ligament and the number of ligaments involved. A sprain can result from a sudden twist, a fall, or a blow to the body that forces a joint out of its normal position. Typically, sprains occur when people land on the side of their foot or twist a knee with the foot planted on the ground. Symptoms typically include pain, swelling, bruising, and inability to use the joint.

Lessons from France

The three most popular athletic activities in France are soccer, rugby, and of course cycling, which is tantamount to religion there. The Tour de France is the country's most illustrious sporting event, and it whips up a special kind of hysteria in people, who do crazy things such as drinking themselves into wine-induced stupors, dressing up like devils, and sprinting alongside the riders while jabbing their pitchforks spasmodically into the air.

I recently completed my first cycling race in France—happily, sans drunken demons—and I experienced firsthand the love these people feel for the sport. This particular event was staged in Villefranche-sur-Mer, a glittering hilltop town on the Riviera roughly 3 kilometers southeast of Monaco, and it was a sight to behold. Local media interviewed participants, dignitaries attended, the course was meticulously wiped free of debris, and racers donned the most fashionable—and the cleanest—cycling clothing I have ever seen. Moments before the start, a French rider gawked at my socks, which obviously displeased him (because they had been previously worn).

That extreme example aside, what struck me at this event was the categorical pride that the French take in their cycling. They have fun doing it, but they take it deadly seriously—even the lower-category riders. The French excel at cycling in large part because they have such a profound respect for it. They know its history, follow its traditions, and ride with reverence. This stands in stark contrast to Americans, who are in desperate shape, Lance Armstrong notwithstanding.

If we can play sports with a greater measure of respect, our performance will increase, and we may be able to enhance our long-term perceptions of physical activity, motivating us to do it more. While

A muscle *strain* is an injury to a muscle or a tendon—the tough, inelastic connective tissue between your bone and muscle. A strain may be a simple overstretch of the muscle or tendon, or it can be a partial or complete tear. A muscle strain can be either acute or chronic: Acute injuries are caused by sudden trauma, such as that from a blow to the you needn't be as fanatical as the French are about cycling, here are three things that will help you give more to—and get more from—your workouts.

First, ensure that your gear is in good working order. In France it is, without question, "better to look good than to feel good." The French cyclists take exquisite care of their gear, and there's some wisdom in that. After all, how motivating is it to ride an old, rusty bike that doesn't fit right or to run in shoes that cause pain? On days when I vacillate between riding and cheese eating, I look at my dazzling bike and know it's going to carry me far and fast—that inspires me to saddle up. You don't have to spend a lot of money on athletic equipment, but you should feel positively motivated when you think about using it.

Next, hone your skills. In France, regardless of how fast they ride, every cyclist I've seen pedals with the graceful fluidity of the pros. It's human nature to gravitate to things we do well and to avoid things we don't. Sharpening your skills will boost your motivation and your performance. After all, if you can cycle with expert form, you're more likely to spare yourself from injury and increase your speed.

Finally, enter at least three organized events every year. You needn't be a competitive athlete to run these races. The idea is that by your setting a more performance-oriented goal, such as completing an athletic event, your standards will naturally rise. In other words, you'll be more inclined to get in those early-morning workouts—and less inclined to eat those circles of Brie.

The following week, I took on another cycling race in Aix-en-Provence. That time I arrived on race day with a deeper respect for the event, the culture, and the sport. And I toed the line in the most gleaming white socks the French have ever laid eyes on.

body or improperly lifting heavy objects; chronic strains are the result of prolonged repetitive movement of the muscles and tendons. Chronic muscle strains are tricky to diagnose, and a misdiagnosis can lead to improper treatment. I had a chronic muscle tear in my lower back for 7 years, which dramatically inhibited my athletic training. In an effort to heal the injury, I stretched the area relentlessly. I later learned that all my stretching had served simply to aggravate the injury. Six months after I began proper treatment—deep-tissue bodywork and ice—the injury virtually disappeared. This highlights the importance of a spot-on diagnosis and appropriate treatment of an exercise-induced injury. If you go with your best guess—as I did for years—you may be doing more harm than good. And the longer an injury lingers, the more difficult it is to fully resolve it.

Treatment for sprains and strains is similar and should be approached in two stages. In the first, the goal is to reduce pain and swelling by following the proven "RICE formula"—Rest, Ice, Compression, and Elevation—for the first 48 hours after the onset of injury. The rest minimizes swelling and prevents further injury. Ice reduces inflammation and reduces pain. Compression and elevation limit additional swelling. Your doctor may also recommend an over-the-counter or prescription anti-inflammatory drug, such as Advil or aspirin. Always remember, in the first 72 hours of an injury, ice is king. Avoid heat; although it may feel good, it can worsen an injury by further inflaming the affected area.

The next stage, rehabilitation, lasts roughly 2 to 4 weeks and is meant to improve the condition of the injury and restore its normal function. To ensure that an injury does not become a chronic, long-lasting condition, your doctor will prescribe an exercise and treatment program that is specific to your injury. The maxim during the rehabilitative stage is "Do no harm." In other words, avoid all activity that aggravates the condition.

Resolving injuries takes patience, expert guidance, and intelligent application of treatment. Take the time to understand the precise nature of your injury, and be smart about how you treat it, so that you can minimize your time on the sidelines and get right back in the game!

24 mph: Learn How to Taper

Imagine this: You train like hell for 10 weeks for an athletic event that is deeply important to you. You've made the sacrifices necessary to put forth your best. When the day arrives, you want nothing more than to wake up feeling fresh, strong, optimistic, and fired up! Instead, you discover, much to your dismay, that you can barely drag yourself out of bed. How can this be? You trained smart, you ate right, you rested. What's going on?

The answer can likely be found in what you did over the final 7 to 10 days prior to your event. In your enthusiasm, you may have overdone it, which left you with heavy legs. Or you may have rested too much, leaving you feeling flat.

When you're preparing your body and your mind for a peak performance in an upcoming event, how do you know how much training is too much or too little?

The art and science of preparing for sports events or big workouts is known in athletic circles as "tapering." Top-echelon swimmers are renowned for this technique. Over a period of months, an Olympic-level swimmer will teach his or her body to withstand, say, 20,000 meters of swimming each day. As an important event approaches, roughly 2 to 3 weeks beforehand, they'll begin to reduce the distance they swim. With 3 weeks to go, they may cut their daily distance to 10,000 meters; then to 5,000. On race week, they may get in the pool only a couple of times and swim a total of 2,500 meters. The reasoning goes like this: The difference between what their bodies knew (20,000 meters a day) and what they swam in their taper (5,000 a day) represents potential energy, which they'll unleash on race day. It's an extremely powerful principle of training—and it's what I want you to do over the next 10 to 14 days.

In the past 8 weeks, your body, much like those of the swimmers, has become accustomed to a certain amount of cycling. By reducing the amount of time you spend in the saddle, you let your body take that net difference and store it as energy. If you taper correctly, your body will reach a physical peak that you have likely never experienced before. It's a thrilling feeling.

Tapering helps you get a maximum return on all of your investment. If you don't taper properly, you will never realize all of that hard work. In this respect, the taper is important to long-term performance in cycling and in fitness. If you can ride at the peak of your potential every 8 weeks or so, it will inspire you to continue with your training—and to reach for more.

Two weeks prior to the big day, reduce your overall duration by 50 percent. If you have built your long ride up to 2 hours, for example, cut that down to 60 minutes or so. Maintain the intensity of your workouts.

In the final week, reduce your duration by 75 percent and perform only one intense workout: the interval session, which should fall on Tuesday or Wednesday. This final hard workout will help to keep you sharp without wearing you out too close to the big day. If your time trial is scheduled for a Sunday, be sure to rest completely on Thursday and Friday, and take a nice short ride on Saturday, including a couple of 10- to 15-second spin-ups, in which you increase your cadence to a high rate without pushing the pedals too hard. This will animate those fast-twitch muscles that propel you on the bike.

25 mph: Ride 25!

This is the day you've been waiting for, a culmination of all your hard work and determination. It is the moment of truth in a literal and figurative sense.

This will be one of the more exciting and inspiring workouts of your life, and you'll want to feel nothing less than on top of the world. Obviously, on the big day you want to feel as strong, fit, confident, and well rested as possible. Here's how to give and get your best when it matters most.

• **Drive the course.** Take some time to drive the course you'll be riding, and visualize how you want to feel every step of the way. This is an opportunity to get clear in your mind how you're going to unleash your best tomorrow. You'll also want to measure 3 miles—or whatever your distance goal is—on your odometer and mentally mark the start and finish.

• **Make sure your bike is in top-notch condition.** Clean and lubricate the chain, and pump your tires up to their maximum pressure (as indicated on the side of the tire itself). You may even want to bring your bike into the shop the week before.

• **Rest well the two nights before.** In the final 48 hours, getting plenty of sleep will help you feel your best. Strive for 8 hours a night, and squeeze in as many naps as possible.

• **Slightly increase your carbohydrate intake.** You needn't eat five bowls of spaghetti the night before your ride to get energized, but over the final few days, you should boost the amount of complex carbohydrates you eat, such as whole wheat breads, long-grain brown rice, and fruit. This will help to top off your glycogen storages so that your legs have all the energy they need to fire like pistons when you're riding 25!

• **Eat a killer preworkout meal.** On the morning of your big workout, eat a light breakfast—a bagel, a smoothie, an energy bar or two, or whatever feels most comfortable. This allows you to digest the food before the workout. Drink 3 cups of water to properly hydrate and a cup of coffee or two, if you wish, to get primed for your event. The caffeine will help to pump you up and improve your performance.

• **Warm up incredibly well.** This is going to be an all-out effort, and you need to prime your body for it. Most people go into athletic events or tough workouts far too cold. You should spend at least 30 minutes warming up as follows: Soft-pedal for the first 5 minutes; then gently increase your speed over the next 5. Stop and stretch your quadriceps and any other muscles that feel tight to you. Re-mount your bike and ride at a moderately challenging pace for 10 minutes. Stop and stretch again. In the final phase of the warmup, perform three or four hard race-pace intervals of 20 to 40 seconds each. This will get your body prepared to clear the lactate more efficiently.

Now it's time to prepare your mind. First, mentally anchor yourself to every positive workout you had leading up to this day. Reflect on how powerful you felt. Tell yourself that you are ready. Clear your head of all distracting thoughts, and take five very deep breaths to oxygenate your body and relax your muscles.

You're ready to roll.

When you feel ready to begin, saddle up and start to roll on your bike. As you approach the start of the time trial, build your speed; when you cross the start line, narrow your focus and get into your zone.

In the first 3 minutes of this ride, pace yourself at about 85 percent of your maximum effort. You should shoot for a rating of perceived exertion (RPE) of 14 or 15. The idea here is to go out hard, but you're to save as much as you can for the latter portions of the ride. In the middle third, build your effort to 90 percent, and in the final third, ramp up to 95 percent. In the last 500 meters, go all out. One hundred percent. This is the best way to approach an event at any distance.

The best thing you can do during the ride is to produce as much power as you possibly can while maintaining complete physical and mental equanimity: deep, calm breathing and a loose, relaxed body. You may even want to talk to yourself: "Stay loose; breathe." Trying to stay relaxed may seem counterintuitive, particularly if you are out to notch a good time; but if you watch world-class athletes during top performances, you will see that even in the midst of great effort, they appear composed.

During the excitement of a tough workout or race, you may forget to breathe deeply. Yet in terms of physical performance and comfort, maintaining a deep, rhythmic breathing pattern during your ride is the most important thing you can do. You must maintain good oxygen exchange throughout your entire sprint.

Late in this effort is where the most attrition occurs. Yes, you want to finish, but please don't risk your health in your determination to do so. If you feel any sharp, shooting pains, recurring dizziness, or light-headedness, by all means stop immediately.

However, if you simply feel fatigue and aches and pains as a result of exertion, push through that. In fact, I have discovered this one incontrovertible truth about fitness (and all organized sports in general): The more you challenge yourself, the deeper you dig, the more richly rewarded you are at the finish and for the rest of your life.

The Finish

In the final mile of your ride, I want you to push past what you thought was impossible. Smash to pieces all of your doubts, fears, limits, and excuses, and break free from those constraints as you soar like the wind over those last 500 meters. Give it everything you've got, but remember to keep your mind quiet. Keep your legs turning over fast, maintain a strong, rhythmic breathing pattern, and dig more deeply than you ever have in your life. Visualize your body literally "lighting up" and blazing forth. How you feel in that moment is the pinnacle of being fully alive. As you scorch the last 100 meters, allow the last 10 weeks of hard work and sacrifice to come flooding back into your veins, and ride as hard as you can right through that finish line.

APPENDIX A: CYCLING WORKOUTS

Level I

The Soft-Pedal

This 20-minute workout serves as active recovery by helping you spin out sore or tired legs. For that reason, this workout is ideal for rest days that follow heavy workouts. It will help speed your recovery by moving your muscles without placing significant stress on them. Focus on pedaling in nice, smooth circles with minimal pressure on the pedals. If you're doing it right, it will quite literally feel like a leg massage. Perform this ride only on flat terrain or on an indoor trainer with almost no resistance.

Endurance

Your endurance workouts are the most important in your training program. They build tremendous aerobic fitness and give you that staying power on the bike, with a minimal level of residual fatigue. Perform these workouts at a moderate intensity, well within your comfort level. These workouts should build up to 2 hours or more. This gives you extra insurance that you won't fade during your hard cycling efforts. During your entire workout, keep your heart rate around 120 to 130 beats per minute. (Yes, that low.) For example, on a 1-hour bike ride, set your upper heart rate limit on your heart monitor at 130 beats, and do not exceed that number for the entire workout.

Technique

This is an easy, but extremely important, session. Improving your pedaling technique is not hard on your body, but it nets tremendous dividends. Cycling, much like running and swimming, is a repetitive sport. Riders pedal up to 90 times a minute, which equates to 5,400 pedal strokes in a 1-hour ride. Therefore, if you can improve your pedal technique by even the smallest percentage, you can realize great gains on the bike. In this ride, keep your intensity low. You should never push past breaking a sweat, and your heart rate should remain very low (below 120 beats per minute), because you want to focus on how you are pedaling instead of maintaining a certain effort. After a 15-minute warmup, visualize your right foot traveling smoothly through the entire 360-degree pedal stroke: kicking across the top and dragging through the bottom. Smooth out any rough spots. Now do the same with your left foot. Next, remove your left foot from the pedal and use only your right foot for a one-legged drill. Pedal only with your right foot, maintaining a smooth circle for as long as possible. This is a fairly difficult drill. It will feel awkward the first few times that you do it, but you'll get the hang of it. After a minute or so of this one-legged drill, clip that left foot back in and pedal with both feet. You should feel a much smoother stroke on that right side. Isn't that a great feeling? Now repeat with the left foot. Repeat as many times as you feel is necessary to ingrain this valuable drill; then warm down easily for 5 to 10 minutes.

Level II

Hills

In this session, ride your bike over a nice, hilly route. More technical riders, who measure their climbs using an altimeter (a device that measures elevation gained), should shoot for doing over 1,000 feet of climbing, but beginning and intermediate riders will want to climb for as long as 20 minutes and as little as 10. No need to focus on going too hard or too fast; the hills will provide all the resistance you need. Instead, focus on pedaling in complete, smooth circles and keeping your breathing under control. Try to remain seated on your bike as much as possible to build extra cycling-specific strength. Cycling in a seated position works your legs much more than when you ride out of the saddle, because you're not able to use your body weight to aid in pedaling and pushing the bike forward. While you may notice that Lance Armstrong frequently rides out of the saddle to take advantage of the position's efficiency, he trains by riding almost entirely in a seated position to build up his pedaling strength.

Tempo

Tempo workouts are terrific for helping build power and endurance, but you should do no more than one tempo workout per week. Here's how to do it: After a 10-minute warmup, ride at a significantly challenging pace—a speed that you could maintain for about 1 hour before keeling over. Of course, I don't want you keeling over! So the tempo portion of the workout should last no longer than 15 minutes. During this part of your workout, focus on pedaling with strength and grace. In other words, you want to ride hard, but you also want to maintain good form on the bike. Also, focus on deep diaphragmatic breathing; this will help you ride stronger and stay more mentally composed.

Level III

No matter what your fitness level or goals, you should only do one Level III workout every 2 weeks. You don't need a lot of high-end speed work to get fast.

Short Intervals

Short intervals are effective at breaking through frustrating plateaus. Start with a thorough 20-minute warmup that's not too hard but still more intense than is typical. You should definitely be breaking a sweat when you're through. Then take a few minutes to stretch or shake out any areas that may feel sore or tight. Once you're warm and limber, do between five and eight hard 1-minute sprints, with complete recovery between each interval. As with all interval sessions, you want the last to be as strong as the first, so be a bit conservative in the first couple of intervals. Be sure to warm down completely after this workout by ramping down your intensity for 15 minutes. At the end of your workout, you want your heart rate to be below 100. While you may be tired, you should feel completely at ease (rather than keyed up).

Indoor Trainer

Rollers (which consist of three rolling mechanisms on which you place your bicycle) or standard indoor bike trainers offer you more benefit in less time, because they don't allow you to coast downhill. As a result, you can shave 1 to 2 minutes off your interval workout. After a 10-minute warmup, do between four and eight 45-second intervals in which you feel like you're pushing hard but under control. Recover fully between each interval.

Additional Workouts

The About-Face

Seasoned cyclists use a common tactic called "reverse loop" to keep workouts fresh. This change in direction is one of the simplest ways to alter the scenery of your workouts without finding a new route. Say you ride your bike in a 15-mile loop around your town or a park. The next time you ride, flip it—do that loop in the opposite direction, and it will look and feel like an entirely different cycling experience.

The Paceline

This workout is done with at least four other people. Begin with a thorough 20-minute warmup before falling into a single line with the other riders. Take turns at the front of the paceline. At the front, the ride is more difficult, because you are facing the wind resistance alone. Ride at a nice, steady pace at the front; when you're ready, pull off to one side, fall to the back of the paceline, and slip into the last person's draft. As the riders take their turns up front, you will move up the paceline until you're in front again. This is an excellent drill for maintaining an overall higher rate of speed while reaping the benefits of interval training, too. Be sure to cool down for at least 15 minutes after this workout.

APPENDIX B: THE GLYCEMIC INDEX OF FOODS

The numbers in the following table are based on glucose, which is the carbohydrate that has the fastest effect on raising your blood sugar (except for maltose). *Glucose is given a value of 100, while all other carbs are given a number relative to glucose.* Faster carbs (which have higher numbers on this chart) are great for raising low blood sugar and for covering brief periods of intense exercise; slower carbs (lower numbers) are helpful for preventing overnight drops in blood sugar and for long periods of exercise. (*Note:* If you prefer to use white bread as your standard, simply multiply the numbers below by 1.42; in this case, glucose would have a glycemic index of 142.)

Aim to snack on foods ranked 50 or below. This will stabilize your blood sugar levels, leading to steadier energy and better weight management. After workouts (when your body needs the sugar), go ahead and indulge in the 50+ foods. They won't do nearly as much damage. These numbers may surprise you!

Food	Glycemic Index	Food	Glycemic Index
Beans		Corn Chex	.83
baby lima	.32	cornflakes	.83
baked	.43	Cream of Wheat	.66
black	.30	Crispix	.87
brown	.38	Frosted Flakes	.55
butter	.31	Grape-Nuts	.67
chickpeas	.33	Grape-Nuts Flakes	.80
kidney	.27	Life	.66
lentils	.30	muesli	.60
navy	.38	Nutri-Grain	.66
pinto	.42	oatmeal	.49
red lentils	.27	oatmeal, 1 min	.66
soy	.18	Puffed Rice	.90
split peas	.32	Puffed Wheat	.74
Breads		Rice Bran	.19
bagel	.72	Rice Chex	.89
croissant	.67	Rice Krispies	.82
kaiser roll	.73	Shredded Wheat	.69
pita	.57	Special K	.54
pumpernickel	.49	Swiss muesli	.60
rye	.64	Team	.82
rye, dark	.76	Total	.76
rye, whole	.50	**Cookies**	
waffles	.76	graham crackers	.74
white	.72	oatmeal	.55
whole wheat	.72	shortbread	.64
Cereals		Nilla Wafers	.77
All-Bran	.44	**Crackers**	
Bran Chex	.58	Kavli Norwegian	.71
Cheerios	.74	rice cakes	.82
Corn Bran	.75	rye	.63

Food	Glycemic Index
saltine	72
Stoned Wheat Thins	67
water crackers	78

Desserts

Food	Glycemic Index
angel food cake	67
banana bread	47
blueberry muffin	59
bran muffin	60
Danish	59
fruit bread	47
pound cake	54
sponge cake	46

Fruit

Food	Glycemic Index
apple	38
apricot, canned	64
apricot, dried	30
apricot jam	55
banana	62
banana, unripe	30
cantaloupe	65
cherries	22
dates, dried	103
fruit cocktail	55
grapefruit	25
grapes	43
kiwi	52
mango	55
orange	43
papaya	58
peach	42
pear	36

Food	Glycemic Index
pineapple	66
plum	24
raisins	64
strawberries	32
strawberry jam	51
watermelon	72

Grains

Food	Glycemic Index
barley	22
brown rice	59
buckwheat	54
bulgur	47
cornmeal	68
couscous	65
hominy	40
millet	75
rice, instant	91
rice, parboiled	47
rye	34
sweet corn	55
wheat, whole	41
white rice	88
white rice, high amylose	59

Juices

Food	Glycemic Index
agave nectar	11
apple	41
grapefruit	48
orange	55
pineapple	46

Milk Products

Food	Glycemic Index
Ben & Jerry's	52
milk	34

Food	Glycemic Index	Food	Glycemic Index
milk, chocolate	34	spaghetti, protein enriched	28
milk, soy	31	vermicelli	35
pudding	43	vermicelli, rice	58
yogurt	38	**Sweets**	
Pasta		honey	58
brown rice pasta	92	jelly beans	80
gnocchi	68	Life Savers	70
linguine, durum	50	M&M's, peanut	33
macaroni	46	Skittles	70
macaroni and cheese	64	Snickers	41
spaghetti	40		

APPENDIX C: YOUR SUCCESS JOURNAL

Make copies of this worksheet and fill out a page as often as you can, ideally every other day. Use this journal to record positive feelings around your cycling and diet.

Date _____

Training

Today's Session Details (duration, terrain, weather, etc.)

_____

_____

_____

_____

Average Heart Rate (or subjective effort level) _____

What positive feelings did you experience during and after your exercise (less stressed/more energized/more confident/clearer thinking)?

_____

_____

_____

_____

What things are motivating you to get out the door these days?

_____

_____

_____

_____

What did you learn about being a better cyclist today?

_____

_____

_____

_____

What mental lessons did you learn today?

_____

_____

_____

_____

Diet/Nutrition Successes

Current Eating Habits

_____

_____

_____

_____

Healthy Food Log

_____

_____

_____

_____

APPENDIX D: BASIC RIDING SKILLS

The following tips will help you master the basic skills of cycling: cornering, climbing, descending, shifting, out-of-the-saddle riding, and drafting. Always strive to hone these skills in your training sessions. And remember: Practice does not make perfect. *Perfect* practice makes perfect. Work on executing these drills with as much focus and fluidity as you can.

Cornering

Successful cornering begins with setting up the proper line going into the turn. Let's take a hard right-hander as an example: If you approach this turn by riding on the right side of the road, you are going to have to make a very sharp turn to the right, and this will feel difficult. Now, if you play with more of the road by riding on the left side while approaching the corner, and you aim at the apex of the turn, hit the apex, and then sweep out to the left side of the road, you can almost make a straight line out of that turn. Good cornering also requires a low center of gravity, so sink your body down when heading into a turn by grabbing the handlebar drops. When cornering, rather than try to steer your bike, *lean* into the turn. Straighten your outside leg (if you're turning right, your left leg would be on the outside) and weight that outside leg by placing pressure on your left foot. This will help to counterbalance the weight of your bike, which is leaning into the right-hand turn. Above all, relax your body and stay focused.

Climbing

Many people believe that you have to have a climber's physiology (that is, you have to be rail thin!) to excel in the hills. While carrying less weight will help you climb with greater ease, you needn't be skinny to be a good climber. Miguel Indurain, the illustrious Spanish rider, was one of the best climbers in the history of the Tour de France, and he weighed almost 175 pounds—20 to 40 pounds more than his closest rivals. Climbing well relies on three things: excellent aerobic fitness, good pedaling technique, and a steely focus. To climb well, you must be fit. There's nothing more uncomfortable than hitting the hills when you're out of shape—climbing has a way of exposing weaknesses on the bike! As your aerobic fitness and power grow, you will naturally begin to climb better. So, to become a better climber, head for those hills! This advice may sound overly simplified, but it's true. Nothing improves climbing better than riding the hills.

Next, because you're traveling more slowly uphill, how you pedal makes a big difference in how you climb. If you have any dead spots—areas in which no force is applied to the pedals—in your pedal stroke, you will effectively stall on the hill each time your leg hits that part of your pedal stroke. When you're climbing, be sure to pedal as smoothly, efficiently, and powerfully as you can. Finally, if you can maintain a deep, rhythmic breathing pattern and can stay relaxed and determined, you will gain a huge edge in conquering the hills.

Descending

The key to descending well is to maintain the right speed. Go too fast, and you're likely to crash; too slow, and you won't reach your potential.

When you're heading downhill, stay low, and keep your hands where they can quickly reach the brakes. By maintaining a slower speed, you can simply feather the brakes into the turns. That will net a better overall descent than coming too fast into a turn and having to hit the brakes hard, causing you to lose momentum. Another important part of honing your descent skills is to know the route. If you are doing a race with a lot of downhill sections, it is smart to review the course before the event. Knowing what's ahead on a descent provides a huge boost to your performance and your confidence.

Shifting

If you choose the right gear at the right time, your cycling will feel easier, you will experience less fatigue, and you will ride faster. The ideal cadence (how many times you pedal in a minute) is between 75 and 95. If you're pedaling slower than 75 times a minute, you are likely in too high a gear. Conversely, if you are pedaling above 95 times per minute, you are probably spinning unnecessarily fast. Shift gears whenever you fall out of that range. It may help to invest in a cadence monitor for your bike to maintain the right pedal frequency. You can pick up a cycle-computer that tells you everything from overall workout time and average speed to cadence and elevation gain—all for about $60.

Out-of-the-Saddle Riding

The French refer to this as *en danseuse,* which roughly translated means "dancing." There's nothing quite like watching a world-class professional rider "dance" on his pedals up a 15,000-foot mountainside in the Tour de France. When you rise out of your seat, you can generate more power, because your legs gain the added benefit of gravity. However, your body has to work harder, because you use more muscle groups while climbing out of the saddle than you do while staying seated.

The key to climbing well while standing is to pedal as efficiently as possible; the tendency is to stomp down on the pedals. If you do, however, you'll stall each time a foot drops. In other words, there will be a dead spot in which no force is applied to the pedals when your foot is at the bottom of the pedal stroke. Try to scoop your feet through the bottom of the pedal stroke to maintain better pedaling momentum. Also, relax your upper body and stay centered over your bike. Pull up a little on the handlebars to generate more leverage. Rock back and forth a bit so that when the pedal goes down, your leg is directly above it. This helps you use the powerful force of gravity. Keep your hands loose on the bars. *When* to rise out of the saddle is largely a matter of physiology and personal riding style. Lance Armstrong prefers to do much of his climbing while standing; his rival Jan Ullrich, from Germany, rarely rises out of the saddle. Find your own rhythms.

Drafting

You can gain up to a 40 percent advantage by riding in the slipstream of other riders. But the art of drafting takes time, patience, practice, and a big dose of courage! The key to drafting is to begin by practicing it at slow speeds and on flat terrain. Get used to tucking in behind other riders. Rather than staring at the wheel of the rider in front of you, you should focus on his or her back. Scan ahead of the rider in front of you, just as you would in vehicular traffic, to anticipate speed changes ahead; and never cross-wheel, which means crossing the plane of another rider's back wheel. If she or he makes a sudden turn, you'll knock wheels and both of you may go down. Like climbing, the only way to learn how best to draft is to get out there and do it.

APPENDIX E: TRACK YOUR SUCCESSES

To stay on track with your Ride Fast cycling program, simply pay attention to the details and derive inspiration from everything you're doing right. Focusing on the positives in your diet and exercise progress can help you to keep going (especially when you feel like giving up).

In this section, you'll find a sample journal page that you can copy and use for every day of your new training program. Spend a few minutes each day filling in the following information, and track your progress over time. Review each journal entry to find out what's working—and what's not—or whenever your motivation wanes. Get yourself back on track!

Day # _____

WORKOUT DETAILS

Activity:_____

Duration:_____

Distance:_____

Terrain/Weather: _____

Intensity: _____

    Rating of Perceived Exertion (1–10): _____

    Average Heart Rate: _____

Benchmark Details: _____

PERSONALIZATION

What physical lesson(s) did you learn today?

_____

_____

_____

_____

_____

What technique(s) made you a better cyclist today?

_____

_____

_____

_____

_____

What mental lesson(s) did you learn today?

_____

_____

_____

_____

_____

How can you become a stronger, more composed, more confident rider?

_____

_____

_____

_____

_____

What positive feelings did you experience during and after your workout (less stressed/more energized/more confident)?

_____

_____

_____

_____

_____

Any nutritional lessons?

_____

_____

_____

_____

What did you learn about yourself from today's successes?

_____

_____

_____

_____

_____

Any additional thoughts?

_____

_____

_____

_____

INDEX

France, cycling in, <u>126–27</u>
Frontal drag, reducing, 105–6
Fuel sources, for preventing bonking, 84–87

G
Garlic, <u>32–33</u>
Garlic supplements, <u>33</u>
Gear
    care of, <u>127</u> (*see also* Bike maintenance)
    checklist of, 1–6
Gloves, 3
Glucose, glycemic index based on, 28, 141
Glycemic index
    how to use, 141
    preworkout nutrition and, 30
    principles of, 28–29
    in sample eating plan, 29–30
    of specific foods, <u>142–44</u>
Glycogen
    depletion of, 85, 86, 88
    restoring, 88, 89
Goal setting, 72, 92
Grapes, red, <u>33–34</u>
Grazing, benefits of, 29, 35
Green tea, <u>33</u>
Group riding, 92–95, 122
Group workouts, 99

H
Hamstring stretch, 19, **19**
Headset, checking, 62–63
Heart rate, importance of, 73
Heart rate monitor
    benefits of using, 72–74
    description of, 73
    for finding ideal intensity level, 104
    information sources on, 76
    selecting, 5
    when not to use, 80–81
Heart-rate-to-time (or –distance) benchmarks, 100
Helmets, 4–5, 50
Hills workout, 136–37

I
Ice cream, <u>35</u>
Ideal cycling zone, 101, 104

Indoor trainer, 138
Injuries
    bodywork and, <u>118</u>, <u>119</u>, <u>120</u>
    causes of, 50, 74, 87, 125
    mistreatment of, 124–25
    preventing, 12, 73–74, 108
    rehabilitation for, 128
    treatment of, 125, 128
    types of
        sprains, 125, 128
        strains, 126–28
Insulin, body fat and, 28
Intervals, 56, 57, 58, 75
    indoor trainer and, 138
    long "cruise," 9
    short, 9–10, 137–38

J
Journal entries, for tracking success, 151–53. *See also* Success Journal

K
Key workouts, 7, 45, 46–47, 48–49. *See also* Breakthrough workouts

L
Leg curl, stability ball, 18, **18**
Level I workouts, 8–9, 10, 46–47, 48–49, 135–36
Level II workouts, 9, 10, 47, 136–37
Level III workouts, 9–10, 137–38
Limits, defining, 91–92
Longevity, best foods for, <u>32–35</u>
Lunch, suggested food for, 29
Lunge, 14, **14**

M
Massage, <u>119</u>
Maximum heart rate
    estimating, 74–75
    exercising below, 74
Medical checkup, <u>43</u>
Mediterranean diet, 27–28
Mental commitment, 41–42
Mental imagery, 90–91
Mental muscle, developing, 89–92
Mental preparation
    for perfect ride, 79–80
    for 25-mph ride, 131
Mind, strengthening, 89–92